Envy
and
Jealousy

HENRY W WRIGHT

Be in Health
GLOBAL
4178 Crest Highway
Thomaston, Georgia 30286

www.beinhealth.com

EAN: 9 781934 680070

Copyright Notice

© Copyright: 2007. Pleasant Valley Church, Inc.

Disclaimer

This ministry does not seek to be in conflict with any medical or psychiatric practices nor do we seek to be in conflict with any church and its religious doctrines, beliefs or practices. We are not a part of medicine or psychology, yet we work to make them more effective, rather than working against them. We believe many human problems are fundamentally spiritual with associated physiological and psychological manifestations. This information is intended for your general knowledge only. Information is presented only to give insight into disease, its problems and its possible solutions in the area of disease eradication and/or prevention. It is not a substitute for medical advice or treatment for specific medical conditions or disorders. You should seek prompt medical care for any specific health issues. Treatment modalities around your specific health issues are between you and your physician.

As pastors, ministers, and individuals of this ministry, we are not responsible for a person's disease, nor are we responsible for his/her healing. All we can do is share what we see about a problem. We are not professionals; we are not healers. We are only ministers ministering the Scriptures, and what they say about this subject, along with what the medical and scientific communities have also observed in line with this insight. There is no guarantee that any person will be healed or any disease be prevented. The fruits of this teaching will come forth out of the relationship between the person and God based on these insights given and applied. This ministry is patterned after the following scriptures: 2 Corinthians 5:18-20; 1 Corinthians 12; Ephesians 4; Mark 16:15-20.

Preface

This booklet was developed from a teaching to a live audience and has been kept in a conversational format. It is designed to reach a personal level with the reader rather than present a structured, theological presentation. Many times the reader will feel that Pastor Henry is talking directly to him/her. The frequent use of the pronoun *you* is meant to penetrate the human heart for conviction, not for accusation. Pastor Henry has been called to the office of pastor, and as such, he takes care of God's flock (whereas one called to the office of teacher does not take care of the sheep).

CONTENTS

A SOUND HEART
IS THE LIFE OF THE FLESH:
BUT ENVY THE ROTTENNESS OF THE
BONES.

PROVERBS 14:30

ENVY AND JEALOUSY

INTRODUCTION

We have learned Bitterness is a principality of the enemy of our soul. Bitterness will destroy our life and sets us up for serious disease.

An area that feeds into Bitterness is Envy and Jealousy, and if you do not get the seed out, it will just grow up again. Rejection is also going to feed Bitterness. If you do not understand Bitterness and Envy and Jealousy, you will not be able to deal with Rejection because this character is banking on the fact that the other principalities he is working in conjunction with, will be able to set the stage for him to come.

Bitterness is waiting for the occasion to come into our life and can engineer the occasion in other people, so that two other principalities can come, or they are there to give him power. He maintains the record of wrongs. Other principalities set the stage to provide the fuel that produces the forward motion which allows Bitterness to gain a foothold. Envy and Jealousy is more aligned with Bitterness than Rejection is. *Envy and Jealousy will take your eyes off God and put your eyes on others.* Rejection will feed off others, but Envy and Jealousy will make *others* your source of value and fulfillment when that source should be God.

Envy and Jealousy has a very powerful dynamic built into it. Envy and Jealousy says, "Yes, what you have is valuable. I appreciate who you are. I appreciate what you have, but I hate you because you have it and I do not." What is so insidious about Envy and Jealousy is that you really like what you hate in the other person.

The problem with Envy and Jealousy is that no matter how much you do have, you are never satisfied. Envy and Jealousy will never leave you alone and will never leave you at peace because *you are always comparing yourself with someone else.* You cannot accept who you are and what God is doing in your own life at your own level.

Envy and Jealousy will keep you from accepting who you are.

If you aloow Envy and Jealousy in you to tear down someone else's blessing, then you are interfering with God. If you are interfering with someone else's reality, you are interfering with God.

Envy and Jealousy says God is not able to provide for you.

Envy and Jealousy *will always make you think God will not take care of you* and He will not provide for you, but Hebrews says,

Let your conversation be without covetousness...
Hebrews 13:5

COVETOUSNESS

Covetousness is entwined with Envy and Jealousy. When we looked up the word "covetousness," for the entire New Testament "covetousness" is #4124 except for this one scripture which is #866. This is a Greek word that is only used one time in the New Testament. The *Strong's Concordance* says #866 is the Greek word translated as "without covetousness, not greedy of filthy lucre." So in this particular case it means without gain. Let your conversation be without regard to gain.

Have you ever seen anyone who is always strategizing for the upper hand? Have you ever seen anyone looking to get the upper hand over someone else in business dealings? Have you ever seen a "con man"? He is always strategizing to gain at the expense of another. That is rooted in covetousness. That is rooted in Envy and Jealousy, *the lack of ability to trust God to meet your needs.*

The Bible says to pay what they ask when you go shopping. If you feel it is too high and that they are trying to take you to the cleaners say, "It is too high; I won't pay the price," which means you are not going to buy today. Now if they come back and say, "Well, wait a minute, I don't want to lose a sale, so I'm going to take off 10 percent. I'm going to give you 10 percent off or 15 percent off." What does that mean to you? You were being conned to begin with. If you walk in and ask the price, ask "Is that your best price?" It should be, since they put it on the sticker. But sometimes it is not their best price. There is a strategy of deception that comes under the mythological understanding of Hermes.

3

Deception is always rooted in covetousness.

There's an unspoken axiom of business that goes like this: "As much as the market will bear." In advertising and in business, it is not desirable to create a buyer's market where they have the upper hand in determining how much profit you are making. When you continually cut your prices, you create what is called a buyer's market. A business strategy that is based on the fact of maximum return creates the seller's advantage.

Now I do not know where God is in all that. If you run a business, rather than trying to bank on the fact that you are going to get the upper hand, you should determine what kind of profit you want to make. Depending on whether you are honorable in profit (which not many people are these days), and if you decide your break-even point is "x" number of dollars and your taxes are "x" number of dollars and you want to have a 14 to 18 percent return on your dollar (your ROI, return on investment), then you would price your stuff that way because that would be the health of your business. If you price your stuff on the basis of maximum return on profit and then you dicker with that, that is deception and that is covetousness.

If I think someone is selling me something at a fair price for the value that is received, I will pay that person without question. If I feel like I am being gouged, this market walks out the door. If that person comes up to me and says, "Well, what do you think?" I say, "Well, I like the product, but I really feel that it is a little too high and I need to shop around." If the comment back to me is, "Well, I'll give you $100 or $200 off," then I'll take it, but I will not argue the point to get it. If I argued the point to get it, that would be covetousness on my part. It is either a deal or not a deal.

In the area of covetousness we always desire something, but covetousness doesn't always involve money. Remember that Envy and Jealousy is rooted in covetousness. If we wanted to create a principality here in the structure of the bureaucracy of Satan's kingdom, we would make covetousness greater than Envy and Jealousy because Envy and Jealousy is supported by covetousness. In fact, if we really wanted to get into this a little further, we could talk about lust, not the sexual lust, but into pride of life, desire, keeping up with the Joneses, comparing yourself with another.

It does not always have to be about money. It can be Covetousness and Envy and Jealousy over clothing; you can lust after someone else's dress. You can covet your neighbor's wife.

> **Thou shalt not covet thy neighbour's house, thou shalt not covet thy neighbour's wife, nor his manservant, nor his maidservant, nor his ox, nor his ass, nor any thing that _is_ thy neighbour's.** Exodus 20:17

You can have Envy and Jealousy for your neighbor's wife. You can covet their "good looks." I have seen a lot of evil, good-looking people in my time. In fact, Proverbs 25:24 says it is better for a man to dwell alone on the rooftop than to dwell in a house with a contentious woman (no matter how beautiful she is). Romans 12:18 says if at all possible live peaceably one with another.

You may covet someone else's healing. You may have Envy and Jealousy because you are comparing your state of disease with someone else's state of health. You may be into covetousness and Envy and Jealousy, but if you are not careful, when you look at that person with that thing brewing on the inside of you, then comes Bitterness and resentment against that person.

Most of Satan's kingdom operates with a networking of realities to produce a final conclusion. It is like building a house. You have the foundation, the walls, the roof. You have this. You have that, and in the end you have a house built on a foundation. If you are not careful you might think you worked this out yesterday and the day before yesterday, but often Envy and Jealousy has an opportunity and that old thing starts stirring when you are looking at someone else.

It may be that you see a family and the man is a good husband, but you are dealing with this unresolved issue of a husband that is not quite so renewed. What are you going to do then? If you are not careful you can go into Envy and Jealousy concerning another woman's husband. You may see a family that seems to be living in peace when you came out of a destructive family, and if you aren't careful, you will get your eyes on that family and start to covet that and go into Envy and Jealousy.

We have dealt with the reality of who you are, not just who the Father is, not just who the Lord is, not just who the Holy Spirit is, but who you are. In creation you are very, very unique. You are no accident, and you are no mistake. With respect to looks, Jesus was not one that He should be desired. Isaiah 53 is the prophecy of Isaiah concerning the physical characteristics of Jesus Christ when He came in the flesh.

> **2For he shall grow up before him as a tender plant, and as a root out of a dry ground: he hath no form nor comeliness; and when we shall see him, there is no beauty that we should desire him.**
> **3He is despised and rejected of men; a man of sorrows, and acquainted with grief: and we hid as it were our faces from him; he was despised, and we esteemed him not.**
> **4Surely he hath borne our griefs, and carried our sorrows: yet we did esteem him stricken, smitten of God, and afflicted.**
> **5But he was wounded for our transgressions, he was bruised for our iniquities: the chastisement of our peace was upon him; and with his stripes we are healed.** Isaiah 53:2-5

In Isaiah 53:2, in the prophecies of the coming of the Lord Jesus as a man, Son of God, God the Word came in the flesh by the Spirit of God. Isaiah described the physical characteristics of Jesus Christ. This is certainly different from some of those long-haired, effeminate pictures with halos you see on walls.

There is no beauty that we should desire Him as a natural man. He had no comeliness. If you wanted to speculate to a degree that would be permissible, you would pretty much come to the conclusion that Jesus was probably not a "hunk." There would be no Covetousness for Him. There would be no lusting, no comparison, and no Envy and Jealousy. He was unique as Jesus Christ of Nazareth, but do you think He had value? Do you think he was a special man? Jesus said very clearly, "I came to show you the Father." He did not say He came to show us Himself. In fact, He said not my will be done, but the Father's will be done, and He reaffirmed that in the Lord's Prayer.

We need to get our eyes off other people. In a restaurant I was sitting at a table, and one of the managers was there. I mean to tell you, if I were ever to select a pastor, he would have been it. This guy was about 6 feet 8 inches tall and looked the part. If you were going to pick a pastor, this guy was head and shoulders above the rest of them. A little voice came to me as I studied this man and I thought, "You know, he looks the part." It said, "Yeah, you are about 5 feet 8 inches, and you certainly do not look that way." What was coming, trying to get a foothold, trying to make a natural thing into an open door? Covetousness, Envy and Jealousy. They came to get my eyes off the One who called me, just as I am, and tried to get me over to a place where I was looking at a man and comparing myself with another person.

I started to entertain Envy and Jealousy that day at the restaurant. I was eating, and here comes the manager walking by. He was heads above the rest. He carried himself just right, and he looked the part; man, what a leader! Saul. The people chose Saul on that basis. He looked the part, he was a head above the rest, and God let them have a man that they followed after their eyesight and not after His Spirit. Well, you know what happened to Saul. So finally after watching this man walk back and forth for 30 minutes, I finally articulated this. I said, "You know what? See that guy over there?" What am I doing now? Falling right into it. I was about ready to get out of the ministry. I was thinking I did not qualify because I did not look like that.

We were also having a conversation about someone who used to be a pastor of mine a few years ago. He was a tall, good-looking dude, but he was so afraid of people that he would come into church late. He had a side door, and he would sneak out just as soon as he finished so he would not have to talk to the people. He would go hide. What a leader! He was full of fear; it was obvious he was just so afraid. He was just tall, that's all. He was a pastor who looked the part, but he was walking in Fear rather than in the anointing.

Well, I started to articulate this thing about this manager at the restaurant and I said, "Hey, see that guy? Now wouldn't he make a good-looking pastor somewhere? Why is he a restaurant manager when he could be right there among the sheep, head and shoulders above them and he carries himself as if he were a general?" I articulated this and the first to respond to me was my wife, then my daughter. They basically told me to get a grip. They rebuked me. They looked at him and within a microsecond looked at me and said, "Are you for real? What do you see in him?" My daughter said, "I wouldn't follow him; he's not a pastor." I am listening to these voices come snapping back at me and they brought that guy down so he did not exist anymore. "No way, we want to follow someone that has a shepherd's heart. He is totally unapproachable, intimidating, good for basketball, but he has a plastic face."

So all of a sudden as a minister, I was comparing myself with someone in the natural, and I was massively deceived.

It did not make any difference in my mind if he was even born again; he was "in." He should quit that job, go find a church, sign up somewhere, walk in the door, and become a pastor. He was it because he looked the part, right? I fell right into it. If he came near my church, I probably would have resigned and said, "Take over. Go for it." Now I was entertaining something very insidious. I took my eyes off the Lord and His appointment, His ordination and His approval, and I started to look at another on the basis of externals. Paul said, know no man after the flesh.

> **Wherefore henceforth know we no man after the flesh: yea, though we have known Christ after the flesh, yet now henceforth know we *him* no more.** 2 Corinthians 5:16

We have to be careful that we do not judge after the flesh.

> **Ye judge after the flesh; I judge no man.** John 8:15

With covetousness and Envy and Jealousy, you are looking at someone else and not wanting him to have God's blessing. The ultimate action of Envy and Jealousy is murder because it wants to eliminate the person. That person represents something they don't think they have.

Do you know what the root is for most wars between nations? Envy and Jealousy. Do you know why the world hates America? Because of blessing. Do you know why the world hates the Jews? Because they are successful. Do you know why they are successful? Because of the covenant with God that He would make Abraham a blessing to many nations.

Do you know why the Jew is successful? It's not because he is really much different than the rest of us. It is because the Spirit of God is on him to honor the covenant with Abraham, and there is a work ethic, although that work ethic has been perverted. That's a real problem because the families have paid a tremendous penalty in relationship. It

9

has become an ever-consuming, raging fire for success. Do you know what I say to Jewish people who are struggling for success? I say, "Why are you struggling? You already have the blessing. If you try to help yourself, it brings a curse. You need to get God in your life and rest in Him; you are going to be successful whether you try or not. You need to believe that, walk in that and accept that."

Envy and Jealousy hates the person that has the very thing they admire the most. I suppose that if we put all the beautiful ones on one side of the room and the unbeautiful over here on one side of this room, Jesus would stand up at the head of the line of the less-than-handsome. But what a man He was! What a man He is!

ROOT OF COVETOUSNESS

We are setting the stage so that you can be free of the wandering eye that produces Envy and Jealousy and Covetousness. Envy and Jealousy is a torment because it is never fulfilled. Hebrews says,

> *Let your* conversation *be* without covetousness; *and be* content with such things as ye have: for he hath said, I will never leave thee, nor forsake thee. Hebrews 13:5

That reflects the Old Testament Hebrew Scriptures.

> There shall not any man be able to stand before thee all the days of thy life: as I was with Moses, *so* I will be with thee: I will not fail thee, nor forsake thee. Joshua 1:5

Hebrews 13:5 is quoted from Joshua 1:5. The Lord hath said, "I will never leave thee, nor forsake thee."

So that we may boldly say, the Lord is my helper, and I will not fear what man shall do unto me.

> So that we may boldly say, The Lord *is* my helper, and I will not fear what man shall do unto me. Hebrews 13:6

The root for Covetousness which leads to Envy and Jealousy is not trusting God to take care of you. It is a form of Unbelief and Doubt and faithlessness. You are not content with what you have. One time I went all the way up to North Carolina to see a man that was the head of a large corporation. I arrived at his house in a red 1978 Dodge Colt to minister to him. When I pulled into the yard, there was a huge Fleetwood Cadillac sitting right in front of my nose. Now who do you think should have been arriving in the Fleetwood Cadillac? Of course – me. After all, I am the man of God. I have come all this way with great healing in my wings, and I drive in, in my 1978 Dodge Colt that gets 40 miles to the gallon. I'm sitting behind this huge, dark blue

Fleetwood Cadillac. Did I feel a little intimidated? Did I feel a little unworthy? Uh-huh. Then out the door comes the guy that I have come to see and he is 6 feet 7 inches tall. "Hi, I'm Pastor Henry, nice to meet you." "Hello Pastor Henry, how are you?" "Fine. Is my Colt okay, parked here next to your Fleetwood?" I was content with what I had – because it was *all I had*. It sure beat walking! Remember, the Lord rode a colt!

Be content with what you have. I want to give you an axiom to deal with Envy and Jealousy and Covetousness: seek ye first the kingdom of God and His righteousness, then all things shall be added unto you.

> **But seek ye first the kingdom of God, and his righteousness; and all these things shall be added unto you.**   Matthew 6:33

Sometimes the worst thing that can happen to some people is to be blessed. If He gave me a whole bunch of money at one time, I probably would just blow it. I may do something He didn't want me to do. There is always just enough when it is time and for me, that's God's wisdom.

You are probably very adept at managing millions of dollars. I was part of a church one time where you could not be in leadership unless you were prosperous and wealthy. The basis of leadership was based on your success. In that church I watched 60 percent of those leaders fall. I have been in churches with people centered around their country club atmospheres, where the ones that had the big families and the minimum wage jobs went down to McDonald's after church and the rest of them went out to the country club. I have watched godliness be equated with success. But the Word says, those who say that gain is godliness, get away from them, but I say unto you, godliness with contentment is great gain.

⁵Perverse disputings of men of corrupt minds, and destitute of the truth, supposing that gain is godliness: from such withdraw thyself.

⁶But godliness with contentment is great gain. 1 Timothy 6:5-6

No Contentment

Envy and Jealousy will not allow you to be content. Envy and Jealousy will not allow you to be at peace. Envy and Jealousy will prevent you from godliness, and without godliness you are not going to have any peace whatsoever. I don't care what you do. I don't care how successful you are. If you don't have godliness as your foundation, it is like a piece of unprotected metal, it rusts. Moth holes appear in the clothing you wear. The buckets you put your money in have holes and the money falls out the bottom on the ground, and you don't even see it happening.

Everyone struggles with lack of self-esteem. We go into Rejection and stir up a whole hornet's nest of lack of self-esteem. The devil is called the accuser of the brethren; he accuses them before God day and night. Maybe you have struggled with your self-worth. At times I do not feel like a great giant. At times I look in the mirror and I do not see Rock Hudson looking at me. I look in the mirror and I do not see that restaurant manager looking at me either. Envy and Jealousy steals your self-esteem from you. Envy and Jealousy accuses you to yourself as an unclean spirit every single day because it will not allow you to be at peace with yourself and accept yourself. It is always getting you to compare yourself with others or to compare your success or lack of success with others, to compare your dress, your looks. You know the list goes on and covers every aspect of your existence.

When you take your contentment, deal with Covetousness and put away Envy and Jealousy, in that day God shall start to have what He wanted from the beginning and then He is able to bless you.

Peace of mind and peace in your heart

We have to be content. The first blessing God wants to give you is your peace of mind and peace in your heart. I have been there, where I felt intimidated when other people walked into the room. Someone would walk in and you think, "Oh, oh, oh." I have been around meetings where all these important people come in with their three-piece suits. Have you ever been intimidated by someone else's presence? Do you know what a man wearing a suit will do in the area of intimidation? He just looks the part, doesn't he? Right there is Fear of Authority and Fear of Man. In the context of Covetousness, Hebrews 13:6 means not having Fear of Man.

> **So that we may boldly say, The Lord *is* my helper, and I will not fear what man shall do unto me.** Hebrews 13:6

Now we have another phylum of evil forces wanting to reinforce this. We have Fear of Man, Fear of Failure, and Fear of Rejection. If you're not careful, in your mind a thought will come that things will be all right when you are just like so-and-so. You are now comparing yourself to someone else..

FEAR OF MAN

I had the opportunity a few years ago of ministering over the phone for two hours to one of the most beautiful, well-known women in the world, and she was devastated with lack of self-esteem. She is a model, and you will find her picture on the front page of many magazines. She is a mother now and is involved with children's rights and children's programs on television. She was a judge at the Miss Universe contest a few years ago in Bangkok, Thailand. She made up her mind she was worth not going the anorexic route anymore. She was tired of holding her stomach in. She

15

decided she was going to be a normal female, but for many years her rate was $500,000 per modeling session. I gave her the spiritual understanding to the battle in her family tree. She ended a very abusive marriage, and today she is very happily remarried. She is a Christian serving the Lord, and she is no longer in conflict with herself. If you were standing next to her, you would be somewhat intimidated, but she would have been more afraid of you than you would have been of her. You cannot judge after the flesh.

Fear of man drives you to Envy and Jealousy because there is a thought that comes to tell you, "If you could be perfect then you would be accepted." Because you do not feel perfect and you do not feel accepted, Envy and Jealousy come to remind you of that, so Bitterness can get a foothold. Then resentment and everything else comes and now you have double trouble. Envy and Jealousy is always fueling the Bitterness against others and always fueling the Bitterness you have against yourself. Ultimately, because Envy and Jealousy represents distrust of God and unbelief and doubt concerning God's ability to keep you, they eventually lead to Bitterness against God. You are the one that opened the door. It was not God; you chose to compare yourself with others.

IDOLATRY

As a human being, as a minister and as a normal guy, I do not make a distinction between anyone on the basis of looks or no looks, money or no money, success or no success. I do not love someone who gives this church five dollars more than I love someone who gives it fifty cents. I do not go looking for people who can give money to this church. I meet people right where they are because God wants me to be with them at that level. I am no more impressed with someone who comes here in a Cadillac than I am with someone who comes here on a bicycle, or hitchhikes if they have to. I make no distinction, because to make a distinction would violate the precepts and allow Envy and Jealousy to come into my life.

Hebrews 13 gives us the keys to understanding Envy and Jealousy:

- **number one, not trusting God**
- **number two, not believing that He will take care of you**
- **number three, not accepting yourself as He has accepted you**

You are comparing yourself with others and other's possessions and situations. Hebrews 13:6 tells us that Fear of Man is tied right in with Envy and Jealousy and Covetousness. You may think, "If I just looked and acted like those people, then I would be accepted by them." Because you don't feel that you are accepted by them and because you don't have all that they have at the level you think you should have, then Envy and Jealousy produces Bitterness and Resentment.

Colossians says,

> Mortify therefore your members which are upon the earth;
> fornication, uncleanness, inordinate affection, evil
> concupiscence, and covetousness, which is idolatry:
>
> Colossians 3:5

So this verse tells us that Covetousness is idolatry.

Envy and Jealousy is rooted in idolatry.

It does not come out of the pure flow of admiration in relationship because there is a spirit behind it. There is nothing wrong with admiring good things in a person, but the thing you admire in another person when you look at them is the very thing you want.

Love and lust produce the same results, but there is a different spirit behind lust than there is in love. The marriage bed is kept undefiled, but outside the marriage it is uncleanness. Lust takes, but love receives and gives. Lust always takes against the person's will, but love always gives and receives in conjunction with the free will of giving and receiving.

If you ever grasp the revelation of how much God loves you, then anyone else loving you will just be a bonus. It will be a bonus because even though you love what other people think about you, the bottom line is if God is "for" you, then who can be "against" you? God did ordain — you shall fellowship together and you shall like each other. You must realize God has accepted you and is jealous over you. You must realize that He has so much zeal concerning you that He came and died for you to make eternal provision for your freedom, so you could walk in it. Then, there should be no question in your mind about His love. You should no longer have any Rejection in your life concerning any issue or any other person. Amen?

It shouldn't make a bit of difference what someone says about you or to you because God us for you. Who else is greater? If you make a person greater than God, you're into idolatry. Esteeming anything or anyone more than God is idolatry.

Anything that you esteem more than God is idolatry.

I've seen women go into idolatry over husbands. I've seen people go into idolatry over pastors. I've even seen people go into idolatry over rock stars or this person or that person. The only person who is eternal is God, and you're eternal only by the grace of God. I want to repeat that. The only person who is eternal is God, and you're eternal only by the grace of God.

If it weren't for God, you and your generation would become extinct to creation forever. The history books of the future would look back at this 6,000 year period and say, "This was the planet of the doomed and the damned to extinction."

If it had not been for the God that created us, came and loved us and redeemed us, we would be condemned to a death sentence forever. God has done everything He ever is going to do to make a provision for you. All you have to do is accept it. You have to accept it by faith. You have to believe it by faith. You have to walk in it by faith. Don't let anyone, visible or invisible, steal that from you.

Envy and Jealousy was found in the fall of man, coming out of Cain and Abel. Not only did we have Bitterness as a strong man, but feeding the Bitterness we had Envy and Jealousy. If you look up the meanings of these words, they are basically synonymous. The Hebrew definition for jealousy (#7068) in Strong's Concordance is also envy.

The definition for envy in the Greek (#5355) is jealousy. So Envy and Jealousy could be very well synonymous. You must guard your heart against coveting anything in another person. You cannot desire it from an evil perspective.

Sometimes idolatry of others also stems from self-rejection. In the church I've seen people be envious of another person's spiritual relationship with God. I've seen people be really pure before God and have that relationship with God worked out, yet other people observe that and hate them for it. In fact, beyond hating them, they go behind the scenes and say, "Look at that super spiritual one over there." When they go behind, not only do they envy the person's relationship with God, but they would want to tarnish it by saying, "Don't they think they're something? Do you see how they hold their hands up in worship? Is that sickening or what?" I've heard people say these things.

We have to be very careful that we don't judge others on the basis of our "lesser realities," which we have all come from. If you see someone being blessed spiritually and growing in the Lord, don't be jealous of them. How many of you have grown in the Lord in your lifetime? How many of you are more spiritual today than you were 10 years ago? How many of you, in the beginning of your journey before the Lord, looked at others who were quote, "more spiritual than you" and were intimidated? How many of you felt lower or lesser? How many of you felt like you were nothing? How many of you came around people who have a relationship with the Lord and shied away from them because you didn't feel comfortable? That's fear. That's not Envy and Jealousy. That's also self-rejection.

Envy and Jealousy can also keep you away from someone. When kids say, "Teacher's pet, teacher's pet," what was speaking? Two things. Envy and Jealousy and Rejection. What about brown nosing? There are those who are looking for the upper edge, and they're looking from a conniving control mechanism. It's manipulation to get an edge on someone.

If I'm walking across the grounds and in an animated conversation with someone else, would there be a tinge of Envy and Jealousy within you because I was talking to her and not to you? Would that be Envy and Jealousy or would that be Rejection? It would be a combination of both. Feeling rejected and then also envious and jealous.

What if you desired a relationship with The Marlboro Man? When you see another female talking with The Marlboro Man, is that an open door for Envy and Jealousy? If you have a high octane ping on the inside, you should get your old binoculars out and look deep because that is Envy and Jealousy. People in this room have the right to be friends with anyone they want to be friends with. If they're not close friends with you, it doesn't mean they've rejected you; it is their sovereignty.

The Spirit of God makes it possible for you to have a pure relationship with people, whether or not they're goofy and regardless of whether they have it together or not. It isn't what they are doing; it's what are you doing.

Someone has to become spiritual.

Who do you think it should be? You? Or someone else? "If they would get it together, then I could get it together. If they would be nice to me, then I would be nice to them. If they would smile at me, then I would smile at them." Wait a minute! What does the Word say? Matthew 7:12 tells us to do unto others what we would have them do unto us. "Well, they wouldn't smile at me. See there, I knew I was just a worm. I knew it." These are the dynamics that are tormenting some of you. This is the stuff that's separating you from God, separating you from others and separating you from fellowship with yourself. You have to have fellowship with God so you can have fellowship with yourself (and love yourself). Then and only then can you have fellowship with others at the proper level.

Remember Envy likes what the other person has but because it doesn't have it, it hates the person that has it. It's a love/hate situation.

Wrath killeth the foolish man, and envy slayeth the silly one.
Job 5:2

Now where is wrath coming from? When you find wrath or anger, where do you find the strong man? Bitterness. "Wrath killeth the foolish man and envy slayeth the silly one." Slayeth. Killeth. What does that mean? Envy slayeth the silly one. It's a reverse mechanism. Envy and Jealousy in action destroys you. It's a poison, but not to the person it's against, but to yourself. I want you to really listen to me. In this particular case this is different than Bitterness. Bitterness lashes out and defiles another.

BITTERNESS

You notice if someone has a new dress on. What do you do with that? Do you think, "Huh, she thinks she is something! Yeah, you know she thinks that dress makes her a better person. I know her. Besides that dress really belongs on me. I looked at that dress with her at Wal-Mart the other day and she went back and bought it. Now I cannot show up at the same church with the same dress she has on." Or, "I looked at that dress just the other day and she went down there and bought that dress. Look at her wearing that dress and now I hate her for it." Is this close to home?

What if in church Sunday the pastor looks down in the audience and tells Mrs. Jones how nice she looks and also how well she is dressed? Someone else is sure to think, "Well, he didn't say that about me." That is Envy and Jealousy, and Roots of Bitterness.

When we were on the west coast ministering one time, we had a chance to visit a couple's brand new home. This was also at the time we had just ordered our new mobile home. Their home was brand new, and it was just absolutely beautiful. We are talking really, really nice, huge, big, open. Well, a group of us met in one of their rooms. It was just beautiful. It was new to them and you could tell she was still working on the decor. I was talking with her privately and I said, "Wow, you guys must be so excited about this house." I told her that we just ordered a new mobile home and were just so excited and she kind of shut down on me. Later on we found out why.

She finally had this beautiful home of her dreams, and it had taken them awhile to get it. But there were people who were envious and jealous over their home, and it robbed her from being able to appreciate and love her home. She felt unclean because she had this and maybe someone else did not. We had to minister to her about feeling unclean and guilty for having this beautiful home that they had worked so hard for. But people were talking and it was just robbing her of being able to accept the blessing that God had given her. She could not even enjoy it.

If you are around people who have Envy and Jealousy, you feel it. Have you ever felt someone else's invisible scrutiny because they were envious and jealous of you? Did it make you feel really unclean? Did it detract from the blessing of God in your life that they were jealous over it?

Envy and Jealousy will bring very serious diseases to your body. Would you like to prevent these diseases in your life? Or if you are developing symptoms, would you like God to be able to heal you? God will not heal you of diseases caused by Envy and Jealousy and let you keep the Envy and Jealousy that is causing them.

You cannot be healed
yet keep Envy and Jealousy.

God is not going to heal you of diseases that are the consequence of Bitterness *and* let you keep the Bitterness. If you have a spiritual dynamic that is not being dealt with, and you do not want to deal with it, you may have diseases that are a consequence of that. If you want to be healed, what do you expect me to do? Do you expect me to offer you healing and let you keep one curse that is causing another curse? Should we sin more that grace might more abound? God forbid.

> What shall we say then? Shall we continue in sin, that grace
> may abound?   Romans 6:1

So in teachings like this I bring the Word of God to your heart. I bring to you exactly how God thinks, and I show you how to apply it your life. Open your heart! Second Timothy 2:24-26 is the Magna Carta of this ministry. The servant of the Lord must not strive, must be gentle unto all men, patient, apt to teach, in meekness instructing those that oppose themselves, or are in opposition to themselves, that God peradventure will give them repentance to the acknowledging of the truth that they may recover themselves from the snare of the devil, having been taken captive by the devil at his (the devil's) will.

> ²⁴**And the servant of the Lord must not strive; but be gentle unto all** *men,* **apt to teach, patient,**
> ²⁵**In meekness instructing those that oppose themselves; if God peradventure will give them repentance to the acknowledging of the truth;**
> ²⁶**And that they may recover themselves out of the snare of the devil, who are taken captive by him at his will.**
> **2 Timothy 2:24-26**

I am bringing you knowledge so that you may recognize the captivity of the devil in your life and acknowledge the truth. When you have received the truth under the conviction of the Holy Spirit, then you will repent so that you may be free from the captivity of the devil in this area of your life. It is important to recognize the problem *and* repent.

I am interested in God meeting every single person, but I cannot make something happen if you are not lining up with His precepts. If you are not lining up with the Word and you are not applying these to your life, there is not a thing I can do. If you do not apply the principles that I am giving you here in these areas of your life, you will not be healed. For God to heal you, He would have to deny Himself to do so. If you want to keep your sin, why should He meet you in it?

Are you blaming God
for not doing something for you?

What are you doing to line up with Him?

I teach exactly what God has said about you and your life and your situation. I want you free. I want you well. I want you to be blessed. I want you to be the glory of God in the earth. I want to give you back to Him the way He wanted you from the beginning, but He lost you to the devil. I want you to be free, and the full focus of my heart is to do whatever it takes, to the best of my ability, to turn the light on to show you — not my opinion, not some psychological mumbo jumbo, not some type of therapy that will Band-Aid you — but the engrafted Word of God which will lead you into all truth and make you free. That is the only way you can go, and that is the only way I am going. It is the anointing of the Holy Spirit to break the yoke over your life. This church was called in ministry to reconstruct you in restoration, to take you right back down to the frame and we will build it back out again. This time we will take away the rust, we will take away the stuff and we will put you back on the road of life again to His glory.

REPENT AND BELIEVE

Mark says that when Jesus started His ministry, He came into Galilee preaching the gospel of the kingdom of God. It says the time is fulfilled and the kingdom is at hand, repent and believe the gospel.

> ¹⁴**Now after that John was put in prison, Jesus came into Galilee, preaching the gospel of the kingdom of God,**
> ¹⁵**And saying, The time is fulfilled, and the kingdom of God is at hand: repent ye, and believe the gospel.** Mark 1:14-15

Are you hearing the gospel? Are you repenting? What else are you doing? Believing! A lot of people hear the gospel, but they do not believe. A lot of people have intellectual assent; they know the truth, but how to perform it escapes them.

Jesus dealt with it very clearly. Do not be a hearer of the Word only, but also be a doer. If you are just a hearer of the Word, you might as well go fishing and get to heaven the best way you know how because you are wasting your time. To *hear* the gospel is not the issue; to *believe* the gospel is the issue.

It's time to believe the gospel.

If you don't believe it, you don't have to worry about receiving, because only those who believe receive. One of the most difficult things in ministry is to tell someone the truth.

When Jesus started His ministry, He started to preach the gospel in the synagogue. He started His ministry by going to where people were assembled and He taught the kingdom.

Henry W Wright

Mark says,

> 21And they went into Capernaum; and straightway on the sabbath day he entered into the synagogue, and taught.
> 22And they were astonished at his doctrine: for he taught them as one that had authority, and not as the scribes.
>
> Mark 1:21-22

Jesus started to teach in the church and there was in their synagogue a man with an unclean spirit. There was an Old Testament saint in that church that had an unclean spirit. The unclean spirit went to church with the man. He cried out saying, "Let us alone. What have we to do with thee, thou Jesus of Nazareth, are you come to destroy us? I know who You are, the Holy One of God." Jesus rebuked him saying, hold thy peace and come out of him.

Where did Jesus say that? Right in the church service. Publicly. Who cried out in the church service? The unclean spirit. When the unclean spirit had torn him and cried with a loud voice, he came out of him. And they were all amazed insomuch as they questioned among themselves saying, "What thing is this? What new doctrine is this?"

> 23And there was in their synagogue a man with an unclean spirit; and he cried out,
> 24Saying, Let *us* alone; what have we to do with thee, thou Jesus of Nazareth? art thou come to destroy us? I know thee who thou art, the Holy One of God.
> 25And Jesus rebuked him, saying, Hold thy peace, and come out of him.
> 26And when the unclean spirit had torn him, and cried with a loud voice, he came out of him.
> 27And they were all amazed, insomuch that they questioned among themselves, saying, What thing is this? what new doctrine *is* this? for with authority commandeth he even the unclean spirits, and they do obey him. Mark 1:23-27

What happened in that church service? The unclean spirit manifested. It spoke and Jesus cast it out. After He spoke to it to come out, what did the spirit do to the man?

Tore at him and cried with a loud voice and then came out. Where did that happen? Right in the church service.

Jesus taught openly in their synagogues. He healed many. Continuing in Mark,

> And at even, when the sun did set, they brought unto him all that were diseased, and them that were possessed with devils.
> Mark 1:32

There are two categories in ministry to others: those who have disease and those who are possessed with devils.

He healed many that were sick of diverse diseases, and He cast out many devils and He suffered not the devils to speak because they knew Him.

> [33]And all the city was gathered together at the door.
> [34]And he healed many that were sick of divers diseases, and cast out many devils; and suffered not the devils to speak, because they knew him.
> Mark 1:33-34

In verse 38 He said,

> [38]...Let us go into the next towns, that I may preach there also: for therefore came I forth.
> [39]And he preached in their synagogues throughout all Galilee, and cast out devils.
> Mark 1:38-39

Mark 3:13-15 tells us He ordained twelve to do ministry.

> [13]And he goeth up into a mountain, and calleth *unto him* whom he would: and they came unto him.
> [14]And he ordained twelve, that they should be with him, and that he might send them forth to preach,
> [15]And to have power to heal sicknesses, and to cast out devils:
> Mark 3:13-15

SARAH AND HAGAR

Envy and Jealousy, which is rooted in Covetousness, represents a major stronghold that reinforces Bitterness. Covetousness and Envy and Jealousy are equal to idolatry and self-idolatry. Idolatry is you looking at yourself, you looking at others, you lusting after what they have, you lusting for it for yourself, and then yielding to Bitterness because you do not have it. You want it and you do not want them to have it.

Envy and Jealousy is the root behind all world wars and all nationalistic strife. The case of the Arabs versus the Jews is rooted in Envy and Jealousy and Rejection. A few years ago in a city I was in, there was a Christian Arab that came from Jordan to minister to many denominations on how to reach the Islamic people. He was an Arab who had the God of Abraham, Isaac and Jacob. What a miracle that is! He is a very learned man who has debated Islam worldwide. He has publicly debated the best scholars of the Koran in the world. At the end of that meeting, we had a little time to ask questions.

I asked him, "Sir, in the great conflict between the Arabs and the Jews, do you think possibly it is an inherited familiar spirit of Rejection and Envy and Jealousy that came from Ishmael, that was passed down, and today the separation is because of massive Rejection and Envy and Jealousy coming out of the rejection?" He looked down across the audience and said, "Sir, your spiritual perceptions are incredibly accurate. That is the root: Rejection rooted in Envy and Jealousy." That is the story between the Arabs and the Jews; they are half brothers with a common father and a different mother. Abraham is the father. Hagar is the Egyptian woman who is the mother of the Arabs, and Sarah is the mother of the Jews.

One of the neat prophecies in the book of Isaiah is about the millennium; the sons of Kedar (descendants of Ishmael) are the first nationality to be restored to fellowship with the Jews and to be restored to the Lord Jesus Christ, showing the posterity and the transference of posterity in the generations. That family breach, going all the way back to Abraham, Sarah, Hagar, Isaac, and Ishmael shall be healed forever. In the tribulation period when the Antichrist is slaughtering the Jews and they run into the deserts of Petra and of Arabia, the Arabs shelter them from the Antichrist, and right there is the beginning of the changing of the heart.

God is greater than you. He is greater than the Jews. He is greater than the Arabs. He is greater than anything. John says in 1 John 3:

> **For if our heart condemn us, God is greater than our heart, and knoweth all things.** 1 John 3:20

If your heart condemns you, if you are fighting a battle in your heart of Bitterness, Self-Bitterness, Envy, Jealousy, Rejection, and uncleanness and unloveliness, God is greater than your heart in these areas and He knows all things. In other words, God is greater than any second heaven influence that has become part of your personality and He knows all things. He knows where you are and His plans for you. He will take you there.

31

ROOTS OF ENVY AND JEALOUSY

We have found that Envy and Jealousy is rooted in not trusting God, not believing God loves you and will take care of you, not believing that you are the apple of His eye, that you are special to Him and that He is able to sustain you in all things of life. Envy and Jealousy is rooted in you looking at other people, and them becoming your point of reference as to who you should be. When you see things in their life that you want and do not have or qualities that they have but you do not, then you hate the very thing that you love in them; but instead of hating the thing that you love, you hate them because they have it. That is rooted in idolatry. That is rooted in one of the greatest powers to feed and open the door for the strong man of Bitterness to come in. This interlocking of enemy forces comes to bring a type of personality aberration. In fact, these things can become so intertwined within you that you can't separate yourself from them. It is possible for you to become so influenced by the nature of these entities that you think it's who you are. That is a sad statement to think that God created you, yet now you are full of Bitterness.

Entwined within all of this are feelings of retaliation, cruelty, fury, malice, rage, sadism, screaming, spitefulness, treachery, control, bossiness, dominance, impatience, agitation, criticism, covetousness, avarice, craving, curiosity, discontent, material lust, stealing, bitterness, anger, antagonism, contempt, contention, enmity, fighting, hatred, hatred of authority (no one is going to tell me what to do), hostility, irritation, murder, resentment, self-hatred, temper, unforgiveness, violence, wrath, strife, annoying, bickering, contention, discord, quarreling, sarcasm, and slander. All of these are entwined within Envy and Jealousy and Covetousness. All of them are moving together like worms in a bucket, and all of them are feeding each other.

Curiosity is rooted in suspicion. The "knowing ones" must know everything that is going on because they do not want to miss out on one little bit of information. That comes out of lust and Envy and Jealousy. For someone to know something about a matter, when you are uninformed, brings Envy and Jealousy. "They know about this. How come I didn't know about that? They didn't include me in that conversation." Looking into other people's business is rooted in not wanting to be left out. It's rooted in Jealousy. This is the type of curiosity that would be meddlesome, "the meddling one," looking for information to be used for future control or perhaps future information that would feed Envy and Jealousy and ultimately create a root of Bitterness.

Sabotage comes out of retaliation and murder, from that root of Bitterness. When you sabotage, you are interested in destroying something of another person's reality in whatever way you can. It comes directly from deep-rooted Bitterness. Envy and Jealousy could be pretty closely entwined within that because Envy and Jealousy says, "I do not have it. You have it, and you are not going to have it either."

When men stalk women and end up killing the women that they are supposed to love, that is a love/hate relationship. Now that she is in a relationship with another man who loves her, that previous man goes into Envy, Jealousy, Rejection, and Bitterness and says if I cannot have her, no one is going to have her. All of a sudden you have love/hate. That is the root of strife and war.

Envy and Jealousy produces the elimination of the person it's directed towards. That's why it is so dangerous. It produces an action beyond the internal thought, because it is not content to sit and just be jealous and envious.

When the root of Bitterness comes in conjunction with Envy and Jealousy, then they work together to produce the removal and the extinction of the person they are directed toward. If you're envious and jealous of people, do you know what you want to do with them? You want them out of your face. You want them away from your presence, and you don't even want to know they're within a thousand million miles of where you are.

What if you're envious and jealous against someone else, and then your friend happens to like the person who you're envious and jealous of. What's going to happen with you? You're not only going to want to remove the person that you're envious and jealous against, but you're going to turn that relationship with your friend into hatred, and you'll want to eliminate them too.

Because Envy and Jealousy is no respecter of persons, it only wants one thing – destruction, without exception. Envy and jealousy is not a peacemaker, and it can never be satisfied. There is no resolution with a person who has Envy and Jealousy. You are wasting your time.

Retaliation is get-even time, which comes out of resentment, which is rooted in Bitterness. I am going to get even. I do not forgive. I get even. I do not forgive, nor do I forget. Or I may forgive, but I will never forget.

If you forgive, but don't forget, you have not forgiven.

Now granted, you remember what people have done to you. You do not lose your memory in this. But when you say I forgive but I do not forget, what you are saying is that you are keeping a record of wrongs, and that is not a place of fellowship. It is a place of suspicion; it is a breeding ground to create the atmosphere to cause it to happen again.

THE PATRIARCHS

The 12 patriarchs in Acts were the sons of Jacob.

And the patriarchs, moved with envy, sold Joseph into Egypt: but God was with him,   Acts 7:9

The patriarchs, the spiritual leadership, the grandchildren of Abraham, were moved with Envy and sold Joseph into Egypt, but God was with Joseph. Isn't that good news? They were envious of their little brother. His father loved him and made a coat of many colors for him (but not for the other brothers). Now with Envy and Jealousy also comes Rejection.

Rejection, Envy/Jealousy, and Bitterness bring a three-pronged assault. Usually where you find one, you find the others. But you can't deal with Rejection, and you can't deal with Envy and Jealousy, unless you first understand Bitterness , because he really is the stronger of the two.

That's why we taught him first, because he is the stronger of the two. He is the reinforcer. He's the one that brings the memories. He's the one that plays the flashbacks. He's the one that plays the instant replay. He's the one that comes and reminds you of that slimeball you don't like.

Joseph also had a dream, and in the dream, it showed his older brothers bowing down to him and serving him, the younger brother. He prophesied that to his older brothers and guess what came? If the coat of many colors hadn't been enough, this young punk – this little kid, looking at big Judah, then looking up at Issachar, looking up at Naphtali, and looking up at Asher and all the rest of them said, "Big brothers, I love you, but I had a dream. In the dream, you get to bow before me and serve me." Now in modern-day terms can you see what the older brothers would be doing with

35

that younger brother today? They would never let him live it down because of Envy and Jealousy and Rejection.

How many people have been subjected to sibling rivalry?

Not me. I'm an only child. I was subjected to something much worse – the Envy and Jealousy of a father concerning his son, because little Henry was liked and daddy was not. I became an object of his wrath. Has anyone ever seen any parents be envious and jealous of their children?

I see many times parents who have failed in *their* lives pour all of their attention into a child, wanting the child to be a success. Why? For the child's benefit? No, they want to be known as the parents of this well-known successful child. Then the parents could have value, and they could have honor.

In fact, they want the child to be the success to replace their failure. Then when the child becomes the achiever, they hate the child. This is a problem I've seen in ministry. Do you know how many parents put down successful children? Do you know how many parents and how many family members do not like it when someone is blessed of God? When a family member is successful and blessed, sometimes others in the family are jealous and envious and will put them down.

These are the dynamics of evil spirits at work in their hierarchy. Those on the bottom are always trying to reach up, and those at the top are always keeping the ones that are at the bottom from reaching up, because it's a caste system. That is coming out of Covetousness, Envy and Jealousy.

In the corporate world, it is dog eat dog. There's no place for mixing different values there. Everyone is jockeying for success, and everyone is expendable to that end. That's Covetousness. That's Envy and Jealousy. Do you see it? It's all around you.

There are people who are envious and jealous of people's success. You see someone driving down the road in a new car. If you are driving your Model A, you may feel that high octane ping on the inside. You see someone with a new dress on, new of clothes, a new home – anything that would be a blessing — and there's that feeling of Rejection, of Envy and Jealousy, of Bitterness . This is life, but it's not God's life.

Well, little Joseph's prophecy came true, and they had to bow to him. They had to repent, didn't they? When they were moved with Envy, they wanted to remove him, to eliminate him, so the prophecy wouldn't come true.

Let's look at Romans 1:28-30.

> **And even as they did not like to retain God in** *their* **knowledge, God gave them over to a reprobate mind, to do those things which are not convenient;** Romans 1:28

Romans 1:29 is a statement about discernment. It's a statement about things that are evil.

> **Being filled with all unrighteousness, fornication, wickedness, covetousness, maliciousness; full of envy, murder, debate, deceit, malignity; whisperers,** Romans 1:29

Where does maliciousness come from? Bitterness. Maliciousness is a form of retaliation. "I'm going to get even."

> **[30]Backbiters, haters of God, despiteful, proud, boasters, inventors of evil things, disobedient to parents,**
> **[31]Without understanding, covenantbreakers, without natural affection, implacable, unmerciful:** Romans 1:30-31

These are some things you might make a mental check of to see if you need to deal with in ministry. If these are things that are common to man, that would not be part of God's glory or His nature, they need not be part of your nature either.

JEALOUSY

JEALOUSY IN MARRIAGE

Let's take a look at the word "Jealousy" for a moment. We want to look this word up in the *Strong's*. The first time the word "Jealousy" is found in the Old Testament is in Numbers 5:14. It is #7068 in the *Strong's;* it is the Hebrew word *qana* from #7065, which says, to make zealous in a bad sense, jealous or envious, envy, to move to, provoke to, to be very provoked, with great zeal. It is to be zealous, but in a bad sense. Now #7068 says jealousy or envy, zeal. In other words, it is an intense movement or an intense reality.

qin'ah, Hebrew #7068, Strong's from Hebrew #7065 (qana'); *jealousy* or *envy* :- envy (-ied), jealousy, × sake, zeal.

> The <u>root</u> of *qin'ah is: qana',* Hebrew #7065, Strong's; a primitive root; to *be* (causative *make*) *zealous,* i.e. (in a bad sense) *jealous* or *envious* :- (be) envy (-ious), be (move to, provoke to) jealous (-y), × very, (be) zeal (-ous).

Do you know how many men are jealous of their wives? I dealt with a man a few years ago whose wife couldn't even go to the grocery store because he would attack her after she left the store. He thought that someone in the aisle was making eyes at her and that she was having thoughts in her heart about someone else. He was constantly making things up in his mind that she was trying to be unfaithful to him in her heart. He would attack her verbally. People at work would call about something, and if it was a male, he would go into a rage because he had a spirit of Jealousy. You will find this in today's world.

Now let's take a look at Numbers 5:14.

> [13]And a man lie with her carnally, and it be hid from the eyes of her husband, and be kept close, and she be defiled, and *there be* no witness against her, neither she be taken *with the manner;*

> ¹⁴And the spirit of jealousy come upon him, and he be jealous of his wife, and she be defiled: or if the spirit of jealousy come upon him, and he be jealous of his wife, and she be not defiled: Numbers 5:13-14

These verses are talking about adultery and another man lying with the man's wife, carnally. The woman could be innocent or guilty. A woman can be considered guilty, and Jealousy will attack her in her innocence. She is defiled by a jealous husband. Many husbands are defiled by a jealous wife and pay a high price because the wife is constantly suspicious of anyone who might have an interest in her husband. Consequently there is a spirit of Jealousy that comes to provoke. It comes out of Fear, but it also comes out of Envy. It is not trusting God. Many innocent men and women are attacked by their mate in the marriage over the spirit of Jealousy. In the psychological community, Envy and Jealousy is not considered to be a spirit, but is considered to be emotions. This scripture shows one of the first instances of this. The Word of God calls it like it is; it's a spirit of Jealousy. *"And the spirit of jealousy came upon him…"*

GOD'S JEALOUSY

Remember the definition for Jealousy means zeal or to be zealous. God is jealous over you. Do you think *He* has an evil spirit?

In Deuteronomy 29:20, it talks about the Lord not sparing him. This is a condition for a man's disobedience.

> ¹⁹And it come to pass, when he heareth the words of this curse, that he bless himself in his heart, saying, I shall have peace, though I walk in the imagination of mine heart, to add drunkenness to thirst:
> ²⁰The Lord will not spare him, but then the anger of the Lord and his jealousy shall smoke against that man, and all the curses that are written in this book shall lie upon him, and the Lord shall blot out his name from under heaven.
> **Deuteronomy 29:19-20**

What this man is saying is, Yeah, I have heard the Word of God; I understand that to take this action can open this curse to me, but I am going to have peace no matter what my heart tells me to do, so leave me alone. What this is saying is a man has decided he is going to disobey God, and he is going to have his peace even though God has said there is a curse coming upon him. In verse 20, the LORD picks up the statement and says he will not spare him, and then the anger of the Lord and His jealousy shall smoke against that man, and all the curses written in this book shall lie upon him. The LORD shall blot out his name from under heaven.

It is a very serious thing when you hear the truth, and you decide that you do not have to deal with your sin issues, that you do not have to deal with your life, and that you are going to have your peace on your own terms. That causes the Lord Himself to rise up against you because what you are saying is this: I am going to have my peace and my blessings and the devil is going to bless me. Lord, I do not need you, I do not need your opinion, and I do not need the discernment. I am going to do what I want to do to bring my peace. The Lord is jealous over you because He wants you. He desires you. He does not want to share you with devils in fellowship. If you have made up your mind that you are going to do that anyway, then He releases you to your own devices. It is all connected with Bitterness.

Deuteronomy says,

> ¹⁷And ye have seen their abominations, and their idols, wood and stone, silver and gold, which were among them:)
> ¹⁸Lest there should be among you man, or woman, or family, or tribe, whose heart turneth away this day from the Lord our God, to go and serve the gods of these nations; lest there should be among you a root that beareth gall and wormwood;
> Deuteronomy 29:17-18

The gall is the word *rosh*, a poisonous plant thought by some to be the poppy, gall, hemlock, venom, poison. There is a reference to wormwood, which is a type of Bitterness.

When you get into the end times when the asteroids hit this planet, one of those asteroids that hits the water is called wormwood (Revelation 8:11). It turns the sweet waters bitter because it has within it a substance that poisons the waters, and causes men who would drink it to die. In the context of this subject of Jealousy, we have the whole movement of individual man, woman, family or tribe: the very essence of Bitterness, Envy and Jealousy.

The jealousy of God would be when you turn away from God's commandments which are best for your life and follow the thinking of the pagan nations. He is not going to put up with it because He has your best interests at heart. In this we see the context between God's care for us and then our type of Jealousy as the comparison.

1 Kings 14:22 says, "And Judah did evil in the sight of the Lord and they provoked Him to jealousy," but it is not an evil spirit of jealousy. It is His zeal.

> **And Judah did evil in the sight of the LORD, and they provoked him to jealousy with their sins which they had committed, above all that their fathers had done.**
>
> 1 Kings 14:22

Do you know what it means to be "jealous over your children"? Do you ever get to a place where you really care? There is a zeal. We went back to the Hebrew word and it literally can be translated zeal. So in the case of jealousy here with the Lord, it is His zeal and His integrity towards us to protect us and care for us.

It is the same kind of zeal that our mother duck has when she is sheltering her little babies. Without the babies, the cats and ducks are buddies. I have watched the cats rub up against the duck because they are buddies. But now mother duck has some babies, and I watched the same cat the other day come up to rub his back on her. She turned around, put her head down and pecked him. Why did she peck her buddy? Normally she would let him rub up against her and she loved it. What was the difference? The babies. Now she has a jealousy, but it's not evil. It's a zeal of protection. Do you see the difference?

That is why it's so dangerous to not take counsel from God's Word when it's given to you. What you are saying is this, "Oh, well, that's for her, but you know, it's not really for me." What you are doing is telling the Lord who cares for you so greatly that you do not need Him. Then He will give you over to your own devices. Paul said about certain people that he was going to give them over to Satan for the destruction of their flesh, that their spirit might be saved in the day of resurrection.

> **To deliver such an one unto Satan for the destruction of the flesh, that the spirit may be saved in the day of the Lord Jesus.**
> 1 Corinthians 5:5

What do you think Paul meant by that? He said he could not help them anymore because they were not listening to God. They were not listening to his preaching. They were not listening to the safety he was giving them. They were not changing, so he gave them over to their own devices. Satan became their word. He became their source. He became their zeal. Satan would be jealous over them, but his Jealousy is destructive because he wants them destroyed. Because they would not follow the commandments, and they would not follow the counsel and wisdom of God, he gave them over to Satan for the destruction of their flesh, that in the day of destruction they would remember from where they had fallen and perhaps they would repent. Even at that point they may have a wasted life, but God will preserve them for Himself in His love in spite of it. Now that would be a wonderful thing for God to do, and it shows you His love in spite of our apostasy and our hardness of heart.

Many people struggle with that scripture and they make it evil. For some people, the best thing that can happen to them are the ways of destruction because otherwise they are

42

going to be lost forever anyway. That is a hard teaching, but it is the truth. The Lord does not want you to go through destruction in order to be saved. His zeal for you is that He does not want you to go to the bottom of the barrel in order to be saved, in order to be healed, in order to be free. He wants to meet you now. But not everyone is interested in meeting the Lord in His love and His zeal for them.

MAN'S JEALOUSY

Proverbs says,

> ^{34}For jealousy is the rage of a man: therefore he will not spare in the day of vengeance.
> ^{35}He will not regard any ransom; neither will he rest content, though thou givest many gifts.   Proverbs 6:34-35

"He will not regard any ransom" means he would not even let you off the hook. People who are jealous are not interested in reconciliation. You can come to them with your gifts. You can come and put your heart out before those who are possessed by that spirit. They are going to eat your lunch. They are not interested in ransom, they are not interested in solution, and they are not interested in reconciliation. They are in a rage. Anger, wrath, rage, Bitterness and murder.

Jealousy is the rage of a man, therefore he will not spare in the day of vengeance. In other words, that person is going to eliminate you if he can. You can bank on the fact that you are an expendable commodity in his life. He will find anyone around him to help him execute you also. He will get behind you, knock on your door, call you on the telephone, and the first thing you know, he is looking for some reinforcements for an army. He will not rest until it is finished; neither will he rest contentedly. The person with this Jealousy that is his rage will not rest contently. There is no stopping this one though you give him many gifts.

Do you know what the Word says about a scorner? The Bible says do not even try to reason with a scorner. Have you ever been around people who are scorners and full of Envy and Jealousy and Bitterness? For every good thing you say, they tear it down and destroy it. You can come with all kinds of antidotes. You can even take the blame for it, and they say, "I knew it, I told you it was you!" You can even roll in the dirt and say "Okay, fine, have your way." It is not enough for them to even win the argument. It is not enough even to be right. You are going to pay, and you are going to be destroyed. I do not care if you are next to God. You have to be eliminated and trashed. God says in Proverbs to not even reply to them even if you are right. If you do, they are going to eat you for lunch. It just gives them more fuel. Everything that you have good to say, they are going to turn it around and make it another evil report about you.

God forbid that you ever admit that you had a problem because that is just the double whammy for them. People who have Envy and Jealousy, and are scorners, are not content just to destroy only you. They will gather to themselves every person who will listen to them, and in a convincing manner they will bring you onto their team. If you have Covetousness, Envy and Jealousy and Bitterness, the spirits in them will find you every time. Birds of a feather flock together. Then you don't have just two anymore, you have a whole flock of birds flying.

Proverbs says,

> ³A stone is heavy, and the sand weighty; but a fool's wrath is heavier than them both.
> ⁴Wrath is cruel, and anger is outrageous; but who is able to stand before envy?
> ⁵Open rebuke is better than secret love.
> ⁶Faithful are the wounds of a friend; but the kisses of an enemy are deceitful.   Proverbs 27:3-6

The Song of Solomon says,

> Set me as a seal upon thine heart, as a seal upon thine arm: for love *is* strong as death; jealousy *is* cruel as the grave: the coals thereof *are* coals of fire, *which hath a* most vehement flame.   Song of Solomon 8:6

Wow, what a statement! Love is as strong as death. Jealousy is cruel as the grave, and the coals thereof are coals of fire, which hath a most vehement flame. Jealousy is a burning, satanic reality.

A person with a spirit of Jealousy is a very dangerous individual. They are not content until the cities are thrown down. They are not content until everything around them is destroyed so that they can stand in their victory. It goes like this: I hate you because you have something I want. Because you have it, I am going to destroy you. The people with Jealousy never get the very thing they want. But because they cannot have it, they attempt to keep you from having it.

SPIRIT OF JEALOUSY

Tammuz was a deity. When you yield to Envy and Jealousy and Covetousness, that is idolatry because you are looking at another as the source of all things. There seems to be some indication that when you are looking at other things or other people in idolatry, God in His jealousy withdraws and releases you to the evil spirit of Jealousy because He will not share you with another. Idolatry of this nature creates a situation where the one that is envious and jealous comes into great devastation. It seems to be that Envy and Jealousy will release you to a profound connection with the spirit of Jealousy with no protection from God whatsoever to deal with it.

When the Israelites were coming out of Egypt there were the bitter waters of Marah, and they were changed to sweet waters.

> [23]And when they came to Marah, they could not drink of the waters of Marah, for they were bitter: therefore the name of it was called Marah.
> [24]And the people murmured against Moses, saying, What shall we drink?
> [25]And he cried unto the Lord; and the Lord shewed him a tree, which when he had cast into the waters, the waters were

> made sweet: there he made for them a statute and an
> ordinance, and there he proved them.   Exodus 15:23-25

The bitter waters represented the Bitterness of God's people in the wilderness. God's provision was to change the bitter waters to sweet. If you change the sweet waters of God, which is the peace of God, when you have your peace with God and when you have your peace with each other without this other garbage, then there is a chance that your sweet waters will be turned to bitter waters. Bitter waters will kill you, will kill everyone around you and will eventually destroy you.

Envy and Jealousy is a powerful inroad for the strong root of Bitterness to get a foothold. You cannot deal with Envy and Jealousy unless you first understand Bitterness. You cannot deal with Rejection in your life unless you first understand this principality of Bitterness. This guy is the superglue that reinforces Rejection as well as the Envy and the Jealousy from the past and makes it a permanency of today and tomorrow. Bitterness, along with Envy and Jealousy, projects to the past, binds you to the present, and projects itself into the future so that your future is as putrid as your past was and your present is as putrid as your past was. So past, present and future, you are locked in the desolation, which is devastating to you. It is devastating to your future, and it is devastating to everyone around you.

Envy and Jealousy and Bitterness are no respecter of persons. They will attack those closest to you, take those whom you seemingly think you love and make you hate them instantly. Have you ever watched love/hate relationships? How can you love someone and then hate them? You did not love them to begin with. It was a perverse spirit that duplicated love. It was not love. It was Envy and Jealousy. It was idolatry. If you love someone, you cannot ever hate them or else you did not love them to begin with. You cannot love someone today and hate them tomorrow. You didn't have love from the beginning. You had lust and a perversion of love which would have been an angel of light coming to counterfeit, meeting the demands of your sin nature, giving you your solutions and your fantasy lust of those needs, and then coming along to destroy all of it.

One of the things I have noticed in ministry is called the unclean, Unloving spirit. It will draw people who desperately need to be loved. There is a perverted spirit that comes into people to create the need to be loved. There is nothing wrong with being loved, but there is a perverse spirit that takes that natural part, magnifies it and projects it, and now we have a need to be loved. Then other people come with another kind of spirit that starts to love on you out of their need. But if you have an unclean, Unloving spirit, it will not let you receive the very thing you want the most, the very thing you need the most. The Unloving spirit will not let you receive it, will not let you keep it, and will rise up and destroy the very thing you need so much. Then you wonder why you are devastated. This is tragic romanticism. If you love someone, you will never hate them. If you love someone and then you hate them, you never loved them from the beginning. You just thought you did.

I have had many people trash me whom I loved, and I still love them today. I do not hate them. Do I have fellowship with them? Do I hang out and become their victim? Do I trash them in Bitterness and hatred? No. Because I love them whether they are good or whether they are bad. But the Bible says to mark those who cause division and have no part with them.

> **Now I beseech you, brethren, mark them which cause divisions and offences contrary to the doctrine which ye have learned; and avoid them.** Romans 16:17

I am from northern Maine where we used to put potatoes in the big bins down in the ground in the potato houses.

They would stay there until the spring when we would go through them separating them by grade. The worst thing that can happen to a bin of potatoes is to have a bad one in there. The seed of that rotten potato spreads and everything coming in contact with it becomes infected until the whole bin has rotted. You have to mark divisionmakers, troublemakers, and people behind the scenes who are trying to stir up Bitterness and Envy and Jealousy because they are like rotten potatoes. That's why God said when you find people in your midst who are troublemakers, people who are causing division, people who do not want to walk in love, and people who are envious and jealous, deal with them, mark them, identify them, have nothing to do with them. At the same time it says in doing so, to count them as a brother, but have no part with them. You love them, but you cannot fellowship with them around the evil that they represent because that would be the destruction of our relationship together in peace.

The Bible says right from the beginning that evil is bound up in the heart of a child. When two children in our home come into conflict, first we separate them and then bring them back to attention to get it together. I will not allow my children to dislike each other. I will not allow my children to have Bitterness, hatred, Envy and Jealousy for each other, and they know it. They are required to sincerely repent. They are required to get it together and make their peace. We deal with it openly, directly and surely in love. Not to deal with it is like that bad potato. In a family, in a church, in a business, in a nation, in a city, if you do not stand up against that, it is leaven that will come and it will leaven the whole lump.

There are many dynamics that set the power of Satan against people's lives. Some of it is very insidious. Some of it seems innocuous at times, but the conclusion is very devastating. *All of our problems that open the door to the enemy usually begin in conflict with another, or in separation from another, or in violation of another.* There are two aspects of Envy and Jealousy: one has to do with the evil side of Jealousy, and the other has to do with God's jealousy, which is not evil.

IMAGE OF JEALOUSY

Ezekiel 8 has to do with idolatry, which is called the image of Jealousy. The image of Jealousy was the image of Tammuz, the god of fertility of the pagan nations who were worshipped by God's people, and in the presence of God's glory, His people worshipped the devil. God released the spirit of Jealousy and Bitterness against them. God had a zeal for His wife (His people). A godly jealousy would be a zeal concerning someone else. For example, a mother and father have a zeal concerning their children.

There is an ungodly side of control and manipulation, and this is an evil side of a parent's concern. Many of you have been exposed to the evil side of a parent's seemingly good will or zeal, and it was very controlling and very devastating.

There was a daughter of a very influential and massively wealthy family. She did not meet the expectation of the success pattern, and she had been devastated all of her life in Rejection because she could not measure up. Maybe she was not called to be a successful businesswoman or even to be successful in a career. Maybe she was called to be something that didn't fit the parents' image. So there was a zeal that came or a Jealousy rooted in Covetousness, rooted in lust and pride of life. I am not entirely convinced that success in the world's way of thinking is God's ordination for our life.

With my own children, I put no pressure on them to be anything. The only grades that are unacceptable in my home are D's and F's. What they are going to be in life and where they will go should be between them and God. It should not be an extension of who I think they should be; it should not be an extension of who a teacher might think they should be. I do not care what their talents seem to be. It is not the obvious that God looks at. He looks much deeper than the obvious.

JEALOUSY IN MALE/FEMALE RELATIONSHIPS

There is an evil part of Jealousy in which a man will be jealous over his wife so that she cannot even breathe. She cannot even look at another man. If she went to the grocery store and the bag boy smiled at her, her husband would put her through the mill for days. He would accuse her of having an affair with the bag boy. In the area of Envy and Jealousy there could be stalking or abuse. Some people might murder a lover or a spouse or someone they are betrothed to. You cannot love someone, and then murder that person because that love is not rooted in a true love, but in a false love, driven by satanic influence.

Not all love is true. Sometimes love can be fantasy lust or it can be based on false expectation, but it is not love. Envy and Jealousy says, "If I cannot have you, no one else is going to. I will kill you and them, if I cannot have you." The papers are filled every day with the reality of this type of murderous Envy and Jealousy. There are spirits sent on assignment. In the Old Testament it was dealt with. There is a Jealousy spirit along with an incredible curse that is set into motion in the area of infidelity. Whether you have repented for it or not does not mean that the spirit of Jealousy has been dealt with.

This is really tough territory because probably 50 to 75 percent of all people have gone into some type of infidelity in their hearts or into adultery or into various forms of breaching the covenant relationship with another. There are divorces, remarriages, marriages that fall apart, and marriages that do not fall apart even if there has been adultery or a breach. Many times if there has been infidelity on the wife's part or flirting or wandering eyes, if there has been that temptation, that looking, that wondering, even in fantasy, even in supposition, then there is a spirit that enters into a man that produces an incredible consequence.

In the case of infidelity, it is very serious when the woman breaches with the man. What about when the man breaches with the woman? It is just as serious, but the man's blessing or cursing over you is of great concern to God. The ability of a man to bless or curse you is very, very, very important, because in the context of godly order, the man has a greater power of permanency of blessing and cursing by his words than the woman does. The woman can set things into motion that the devil will use, but when the husband or the father or the man makes a declaration, or a statement of intent enters into his heart, it has greater power with it for spiritual abuse than the woman has in the same area.

RESPONSIBILITY OF HUSBAND/FATHER

Numbers states, according to the law, that if a man is married and he, standing by, hears his wife bind her soul to a curse, if he allows her words to stand, then she has bound her soul to the curse and the consequences of that curse. He also binds himself to that same curse in his own life. But if he hears his wife bind her soul to a curse and disallows it saying, "Dear, I do not think those words or those actions are really what you mean and your thinking is incorrect here. I think it could be a curse to you and to me. I cannot allow this thought to continue. I'll give you the chance to repent and get this changed." If he does that and disallows her words, then she is free of that curse and he is free also.

> ⁶And if she had at all an husband, when she vowed, or uttered ought out of her lips, wherewith she bound her soul;
> ⁷And her husband heard *it,* and held his peace at her in the day that he heard *it:* then her vows shall stand, and her bonds wherewith she bound her soul shall stand.
> ⁸But if her husband disallowed her on the day that he heard *it;* then he shall make her vow which she vowed, and that which she uttered with her lips, wherewith she bound her soul, of none effect: and the LORD shall forgive her.
> Numbers 30:6-8

In the case of the daughter, if the father hears his daughter bind her soul to a curse and standing by allows it and does not interfere, then he has allowed his daughter to bind her soul to a curse, and he has bound himself to the same curse his daughter is bound to. But if he is standing by hearing his daughter binding her soul to a curse and disallows it, he has freed his daughter from the curse and has freed himself from the curse.

> ³If a woman also vow a vow unto the LORD, and bind herself by a bond, *being* in her father's house in her youth;
> ⁴And her father hear her vow, and her bond wherewith she hath bound her soul, and her father shall hold his peace at her:

> then all her vows shall stand, and every bond wherewith she
> hath bound her soul shall stand.
>
> ⁵But if her father disallow her in the day that he heareth; not
> any of her vows, or of her bonds wherewith she hath bound
> her soul, shall stand: and the LORD shall forgive her, because
> her father disallowed her.   Numbers 30:3-5

There is no provision for men or male children. There is
no provision because the male and the male child is
supposed to be correct in all spiritual things at all times as
far as God is concerned.

> If a man vow a vow unto the LORD, or swear an oath to bind
> his soul with a bond; he shall not break his word, he shall do
> according to all that proceedeth out of his mouth.
>   Numbers 30:2

Now you see how far we have fallen. It is as much a sin
to commit adultery as it is to produce strife. There are no
degrees of sin. There is only one unpardonable sin, and all
sin is sin. The Bible says that under the law if you are guilty
of one article of the law, you are guilty of all, and there is no
provision for partial freedom.

> For whosoever shall keep the whole law, and yet offend in
> one *point*, he is guilty of all.   James 2:10

The spiritual dynamics are incredible concerning the
impact of a spirit of Jealousy in your life from a husband, or
a past husband if you are divorced, or possibly even a past
lover. When a man has had relations with a harlot, he
becomes one with her. We call that a soul tie or the
transference of unclean spirits. Yet in the Word it says that if
a man looks upon a woman and he takes her in his heart, he
has committed adultery within his heart. This is not just the
temptation of adulterous relations, but the completeness of
an action within the heart.

But I say unto you, That whosoever looketh on a woman to lust after her hath committed adultery with her already in his heart. Matthew 5:28

The spirit of Jealousy will produce destructive forces against you all your days and keep you from your freedom emotionally and sexually. It may be even keeping you from the restoration of your marriage because the forces are very strong. Bitterness is a strong principality along with the power and the spirits that answer to it. Envy and Jealousy includes Covetousness. Have you ever heard the scripture not to covet your neighbor's wife?

Numbers tells us about the law of Jealousy, what the Old Testament church did, and how they dealt with it. In the midst of this, there is an incredible curse of disease. You may need to be released from the powerful curse of Jealousy from a husband or from a past husband or whatever, but also released to health. If there is any validity to infidelity in your life at any point, there is an incredible curse that comes. No one is under indictment here. No one has to feel unclean. You feel like if it has happened in your life so that you have to feel ashamed. Do not go into pride. Do not go into denial. Come before the Lord in honesty and integrity and present your heart before Him. You will find He is gracious. Many of you are struggling with spiritual problems in your life. This could be a major key to unraveling God's mercy to you. One thing I know about God, He wants you to take responsibility. When you do, it means you have the spiritual dynamics straightened out in your heart.

Numbers says,

> ¹¹And the LORD spake unto Moses, saying,
> ¹²Speak unto the children of Israel, and say unto them, If any man's wife go aside, and commit a trespass against him,
> ¹³And a man lie with her carnally, and it be hid from the eyes of her husband, and be kept close, and she be defiled, and *there be* no witness against her, neither she be taken *with the manner;*

> **14**And the spirit of jealousy come upon him, and he be jealous of his wife, and she be defiled: or if the spirit of jealousy come upon him, and he be jealous of his wife, and she be not defiled: Numbers 5:11-14

This is a statement of a man with a spirit of Jealousy coming into him concerning his wife and two realities are being discussed: whether or not she has gone into a sexual relationship with another man. The spirit of Jealousy can come into a man, yet the woman can be innocent. The spirit of Jealousy can come into the man and the woman can be guilty. There was a way of dealing with this in the Old Testament and it was pretty tough.

If the spirit of Jealousy was to come upon the man, Numbers says,

> Then shall the man bring his wife unto the priest, and he shall bring her offering for her, the tenth *part* of an ephah of barley meal; he shall pour no oil upon it, nor put frankincense thereon; for it *is* an offering of jealousy, an offering of memorial, bringing iniquity to remembrance. Numbers 5:15

It will be God who judges the woman guilty or not guilty, whether or not she has been caught or not caught, whether or not she is innocent or she is guilty.

> **16**And the priest shall bring her near, and set her before the LORD:
> **17**And the priest shall take holy water in an earthen vessel; and of the dust that is in the floor of the tabernacle the priest shall take, and put *it* into the water:
> **18**And the priest shall set the woman before the LORD, and uncover the woman's head, and put the offering of memorial in her hands, which *is* the jealousy offering: and the priest shall have in his hand the bitter water that causeth the curse:
> **19**And the priest shall charge her by an oath, and say unto the woman, If no man have lain with thee, and if thou hast not gone aside to uncleanness *with another* instead of thy husband, be thou free from this bitter water that causeth the curse:

²⁰But if thou hast gone aside *to another* instead of thy husband, and if thou be defiled, and some man have lain with thee beside thine husband:

²¹Then the priest shall charge the woman with an oath of cursing, and the priest shall say unto the woman, The LORD make thee a curse and an oath among thy people, when the LORD doth make thy thigh to rot, and thy belly to swell;

Numbers 5:16-21

The curse coming out of this infidelity is not just adultery anymore. We are not dealing with adultery; we are dealing with the spirit of Jealousy and the consequences of it coming into a woman from her husband. If she were guilty, some of the physical maladies that came were that her thigh would rot and her belly would swell and this water that causes the curse should go into her bowels. Now we are dealing with intestinal problems. Into thy bowels to make thy belly to swell, and thy thigh to rot. The woman shall say, Amen, Amen. So be it, so be it.

The priest shall write these curses in a book...

²²And this water that causeth the curse shall go into thy bowels, to make *thy* belly to swell, and *thy* thigh to rot: And the woman shall say, Amen, amen.

²³And the priest shall write these curses in a book, and he shall blot *them* out with the bitter water:

²⁴And he shall cause the woman to drink the bitter water that causeth the curse: and the water that causeth the curse shall enter into her, *and become* bitter.

²⁵Then the priest shall take the jealousy offering out of the woman's hand, and shall wave the offering before the LORD, and offer it upon the altar:

²⁶And the priest shall take an handful of the offering, *even* the memorial thereof, and burn *it* upon the altar, and afterward shall cause the woman to drink the water.

²⁷And when he hath made her to drink the water, then it shall come to pass, *that,* if she be defiled, and have done trespass against her husband, that the water that causeth the curse shall enter into her, *and become* bitter, and her belly shall swell, and her thigh shall rot: and the woman shall be a curse among her people.

> [28]And if the woman be not defiled, but be clean; then she shall be free, and shall conceive seed.   Numbers 5:22-28

One of the key things in marriage and one of the key things that I deal with in my life is that Donna is not, first of all, my wife. Do you know who she is? No, she's not my friend first either. She's my sister in the Lord. When you go back to the Song of Solomon, you'll find it right there. Solomon 4:9 says, "My sister, my spouse," not in the incestual concept, but in the family of God concept. Donna is my sister in the Lord, and because of that she belongs to the Lord before she belongs to me. That's number one. Number two is that she is a friend of the Lord, and I'm not going to mess with the Lord's friend! She's a friend to Jesus. She's my sister. We have a common Father which is God. Together we will have a common husband, mystically speaking, in the future. We'll serve Him together. She's his friend, and she's the daughter of my Father. Then and only then are we friends. I cannot be any greater friend to her than I am a friend to Jesus. I cannot be anything more to you than I already have happening between me and God. That's the best I can be to you as a friend. Those things that are in my life because it's not right between me and God are the same things that separate me from my friendship with you. Are you getting the picture?

One of the things I read on the success of marriages from the world's perspective is very scriptural. Actually it was in *Ladies' Home Journal.* I was amazed to see it in the secular context because churches don't even teach it. It said that the greatest marriage relationship is based on the husband becoming a better friend to the wife than her girlfriends are. The success of a marriage depends on her looking to her husband as her friend, not to the women around her. All successful marriages were studied from a psychological humanistic standpoint strictly based on polls and interviews. In the successful ones, the women, without exception, said, "My husband is my best friend." I've taught that for years, and I read it in a 1997 in *Ladies' Home Journal*. What a confirmation!

This is not a marriage seminar, but husbands need to hear this too. All you ladies who are married can get a tape and send it to your husband and stick it under his nose, and say, "Donna makes him read *Ladies' Home Journal*. So here, listen to Pastor."

Now *Ladies' Home Journal* is not always correct, but in this particular case the observation was correct because Jesus said to his bride, "I no longer call you servants; I call you friends." That statement is from your eternal mystical future husband to you, as His bride, to whom He's betrothed. He is saying to you, "Wife, you're my friend." In the spiritual, mystical understanding, you look up to Heaven to your husband, the Lord, and you say, "I like you too, friend." As you bring the flow of the spiritual dynamics of friendship with you and God, then it comes right down to the horizontal level.

What does Envy and Jealousy try to do? Destroy this atmosphere. Oh it's profound. It's accurate. It's your struggle. It's your battle. These invisible entities assigned against you in your generations and your personal lives know how to work you over, and they do it right between your ears. They use your five physical senses of what you see and observe, usually without your knowledge, and project conclusions into your mind that are usually faulty. Then you draw conclusions based on faulty information and make it truth in your life. That's where Bitterness, Envy and Jealousy, and Rejection get a foothold. You're making decisions based on error and on physical observation that may not be true.

You know the thoughts that pierce you when you make an observation at any level, don't you? Do you know what you're struggling with? You have to decide if it is temptation or if it is part of your nature. Have these critters, these parasites, already become part of your nature and part of your spiritual dynamics? Do they exist or is this just temptation? I promise you that you are able to answer that if you're honest with yourself.

Envy and Jealousy will kill you. Isn't that what Job said? Envy slayeth the silly one. What did Proverbs say about Jealousy? It is the rottenness of the bones. Don't be envious of anyone else. Don't allow the enemy to put Rejection and Envy and Jealousy in you. If you see a person you like hanging out with someone else instead of you, and if you feel this high octane ping on the inside, that is Envy and Jealousy. It will lead to Bitterness and hatred, and that is sin to you. I don't care what you say about it. That is sin to you. It will bring a curse on your head until it's dealt with. Now I just gave you a good diagnosis for freedom and for health, didn't I?

BARRENNESS

This is the law of Jealousy and possibly in the area of barrenness, there is an inherited infidelity in the family tree that was never dealt with. Where does the curse of barrenness come from and why? Right here in this one scripture it seems to be if the woman would be innocent, then she shall be released to conceive.

This is the law of Jealousy...

> ²⁹This *is* the law of jealousies, when a wife goeth aside *to another* instead of her husband, and is defiled;
> ³⁰Or when the spirit of jealousy cometh upon him, and he be jealous over his wife, and shall set the woman before the LORD, and the priest shall execute upon her all this law.
> ³¹Then shall the man be guiltless from iniquity, and this woman shall bear her iniquity.   Numbers 5:29-31

We are not under the law according to Scripture. Jesus did not come to do away with the law, but that the law through Him might be fulfilled. The great news about what Christ did for you at the cross is that in your generation, whether this is inherited or in your own life, you can be free of this today and free from the consequences of it. There may be a curse of Jealousy operating against females in the area of Jealousy from a husband. Maybe he did do something to cause you to go into infidelity. He may have failed you a thousand ways. Maybe you did this in your heart instead of actually going to bed with another man, but you need to come before the Lord and deal with it. It is possible to deal with the spirit of Jealousy that could be against your life producing the disease.

In our family tree and in our life, we need to come before the Lord and deal with it. Many people are so filled with guilt about the past and infidelity that they make infidelity to be the greatest of all sins, and it is not. Every sin has its consequences and every sin produces the ability for Satan to rule and produce disease in your bodies and afflict your souls. This may not be painless in your heart to look at, but it is time to come before the Lord and deal with it. Not just AC, but BC; not just after you accepted Christ, but before you accepted Christ. You may have entered into situations where there was open knowledge of infidelity and adultery. You know your husband knew it. You have talked about it, and maybe you have your healing now, but is the spirit of Jealousy broken over the man? That is the question. Is there something that is ruling? Is there a power that is set against you? Is that power set to even drive you further and further away from the resolution? We are dealing with the spirit of Envy and Jealousy, and there is a side to it that could be very evil.

PRAYER - ENVY AND JEALOUSY

Father God, we come to you in the name of Jesus. All have sinned and come short of the glory of God. In my generations, there is probably some evidence of a reason for Jealousy to be in the heart of a man concerning the woman in my family tree, either through open adultery or through just looking and setting in motion those things that are lust and fantasy. Father, even if there was no sexual act consummated, no unfaithfulness, no adultery, no fornication, nothing even completed in the heart, I take responsibility for it.

I ask You to forgive my ancestors. I ask You to forgive me for the weakness of the flesh that would be there. I forgive my husband for the spirit of Jealousy, and at the same time I ask You to forgive me for setting things into motion that would have given the spirit of Jealousy the right to rule my husband. I repent to You for my weakness and for my lack of covenant regardless, if there was an excuse or not. Before you Father, there is no reason, and so I would take the position that all weakness in my life in this area would have been sin. Spirits entered that would come to take advantage of this situation.

I repent and ask You to forgive my ancestors for the curse of infidelity back ten generations. I ask that I be released from the spirit of Jealousy that may be on assignment against me today trying to complete its mission and to create a breach.

I ask to be released from the bitter waters that may be plaguing my soul, that may be causing my innards to be afflicted, causing my intestinal tract to be diseased, causing any problem in the gastrointestinal tract, any swelling of the belly, rottenness of the thighs, rottenness of my bones, the consequences of the unresolved issues that are the result of the spirit of Jealousy that may be assigned against me. Father, I ask that You forgive me and deliver me. I repent, not only for my family tree, but for myself. I take responsibility so that the penalty for the curse of Jealousy can be broken over my life. For whatever reason, I take responsibility for it now, in the past, and in the future. The Word says that the spirit is strong, but the flesh is weak, and in my days either as a Christian or a non-christian, I may have opened the door for the spirit of Jealousy to come into my husband and for that I repent to You.

Father, if there be an evil spirit of Jealousy that came upon my husband, yet I was innocent, I ask to be released because I am not guilty and the Word says, "The curse causeless shall not come." So in the name of Jesus, the provision for freedom from the spirit of Jealousy and the bitter waters and the swelling of the belly and the rottenness of the thighs, I ask to be delivered and healed today. Satan, you have no right to my life. Father, I thank You for Your provision. Amen.

If you are in agreement, go before the Lord, scan through your past and get this thing straight with God right now. With any temptation in the area of adultery, take this time in your heart right now. Take this time to get it right.

BORN OUT OF WEDLOCK

Concerning people who have been born out of wedlock, there is a spirit of Jealousy that rules the husband of the woman coming out of adulterous situations.

There is a spirit of Jealousy that not only goes down to the mother in infidelity, but when there is a child birthed out of the sexual relationship, there sometimes is a spirit of Jealousy that travels from that husband and attaches itself to the child. It doesn't come from the biological father; it comes from the father of the first covenant (the husband).

There could be a spirit of Jealousy that would come into that child that was coming out of the adulterous affair or out of that situation.

JEALOUSY FROM OTHERS

There is another situation—sometimes people are plagued by others being jealous of them. There could be this type of breach in the family tree somewhere or a personal life circumstance where the spirit of Jealousy is running across a broad spectrum of humanity's problems, relationships and interrelationships. There can be Jealousy for others, like a Jealousy from woman to woman, or competition. Females competing with other females for male approval is a big one. There is never a secure feeling. Sometimes that can come out of Rejection by a father; sometimes that can come out of Rejection by a mother, but a lot of times it can come out of Jealousy. That is what produces cat fights. In the world, the girls would go out and start fighting for some guy that they really had their eye on, and there would be a cat fight out in the parking lot if they had consumed too much beer. Some of that could have its root in the spirit of Jealousy coming out of insecurity, but the point is, when you have this, you have insecurity. You do not have a standard; you do not have a foundation of trust.

As you go before the Lord, take time to get your heart right concerning yourself and concerning your own past, your own life, and your family tree. In your heart, make your peace with God about this. If you have to repent to someone in your heart, do it. You may not necessarily have to go back to the husband or the ex-husband, and repent. But you have to take responsibility for feeding and causing the spirit of Jealousy.

If you are innocent, then the Word makes provision for you. You do not have to worry about it. You may be innocent, but you may be plagued with temptation that is coming because of your mother or your grandmother or someone in your family tree that did have that problem. So if you are still innocent, but you are plagued with dipping into guilt and fantasy or the potential of infidelity, I would suggest very strongly that you consider that a spirit of Jealousy might be working in your family tree and you would need to come and understand that also. When things come into your mind or things plague you and torment you with temptation, you need to pay very close attention to when it came into your inherited family tree. Just recognize there may be a spirit of Jealousy working in your family tree and ask God to deliver you from it. You may be innocent, but it does not mean you aren't plagued by the inherited spirits that have come rolling through. A lot of you are victims of your generations and you are struggling. Although it really was not your sin, there is always a temptation there, and it is trying to roll itself over; there is a conflict. You are a victim somewhere.

A lot of people say, "This is not fair. Why should I pay the price for my ancestors?" Because God said you would. Why? So that you could get it straight and prevent future generations from going through the same thing you did. We must get the curse so well broken in your generation that your children can be delivered too. We have to face it on the basis of how God has taught us. The wages of sin is death; this has not changed. Just come before God and take your freedom today. This is not a time to go into guilt, this is a time to come and get your freedom, so that the spirit of Jealousy can be broken. You may be liberated to a greater personal relationship with a husband or a mate in the future.

This is a very serious thing. It is close to God's heart and is one of the ordinances of the Old Testament church that had a very significant spiritual implication. What you have to repent for is any type of relationship where there has been infidelity or a person may have had Jealousy. First of all, if you are in fornication, you are breaking law number one. Number two is that even in breaking law number one you can set additional dynamics in motion because there are people who are unfaithful even in "illegal" relationships.

Everything has a dynamic, everything has a consequence, and you can have someone in that situation with a spirit of Jealousy.

Many beautiful Christian girls start going out with ungodly men or marry ungodly men. There is usually a spirit of Jealousy in that man concerning that woman. In our own life we had to decide we would not compromise God concerning a daughter. We laid her on the altar and decided to serve God. That is what broke it. But that individual was an ungodly boy, and he was full of evil. He was full of Jealousy, and he was the kind of guy that would have killed if he could not have her. God was with us, and today she is happy. We all learned a wonderful lesson. But if we had not been spiritual, if we had not had the Word of God, would there have been consequences with our daughter? Absolutely. It took us several months to get her clear of the transference of spirits that came, in such a way that we did not have a breach between ourselves.

You need to be liberated to a pure relationship with a man, but not just with a man because there is a lot of cross-sectioning here of Jealousy in females too, over the very same issue. The spirit of Jealousy needs to be broken. You need to be released from any curses that are flying because Proverbs says,

> **As the bird by wandering, as the swallow by flying, so the curse causeless shall not come.** Proverbs 26:2

If there is any evidence of this curse having a cause to come to your life or because of your family tree, this is a wonderful time to come before the Lord and get it broken. I believe God will honor you according to the integrity of your heart. Just come before God with a sincere, humble heart about these issues.

Have you taken responsibility for the iniquities of your ancestors and your life?

You do not have any right to hate Jesus' friends. Now if you want to mess with the Lord's friends, you go right ahead, but do you know who the Lord is going to defend? His friends. Wait a minute! You're a friend of the Lord, too, aren't you? The Word says you are. Jesus said in John 15:5, "I no longer call you servants but I call you friends." So if you are a friend to Jesus and Jesus is a friend of yours, then who else is a friend of Jesus? Everyone else is a friend of Jesus, and Jesus is their friend. Do you want to mess with Jesus' friend? If you do, then you mess with Him. He is not going to defend you. He is going to defend His friends who are abiding in Him. You open yourself up to an area of breach with the Lord when you touch those He loves. Do you think the Lord would defend you if someone touched you, and you were his friend? Oh, absolutely. Guard your heart. Guard your mind. Guard your tongue. Guard your soul. Don't mess with Jesus' friends.

PRAYER OVER FAMILY TREE

Father, according to every man's faith and every woman's faith, and the integrity of their heart, I ask that Your mercy and Your grace be extended so the curse be cancelled. Lord, one of the reasons that You came to bear the curse at this level is so that we could be free. Father, according to the righteousness of their hearts, according to the convictions of their hearts, according to the dedication before You this day, in the name of the Lord Jesus Christ, I take authority over the spirit of Jealousy back into every generation because it needs to be broken at all levels.

I release you to your freedom in the Lord Jesus Christ, without shame, without guilt, and without the pressures that this spirit of Jealousy would produce in your life. I release you from the spirits of infirmity that would plague your gastrointestinal tracts, that would cause the swelling of the belly and that would put a rottenness in your thigh, in the name of the Lord Jesus. I speak to the spirits of infirmity that would be on assignment against anyone in the name of the Lord Jesus Christ, and I release you from your assignment. Father, I ask that You raise everyone up in healing, that You deliver them, and that You heal them here today. All the people said Amen, Amen, Amen.

Did you feel an absolute release in your spirit from the bondage and pressure of Envy and Jealousy? The spirit of Jealousy at this level is incredibly evil because it is right there all the time. Even in the area of competition, it is right there all the time. It is always there, working, working, working in the area of Jealousy.

JEALOUSY OF THE LORD

There is a jealousy of the Lord for you when you are in spiritual harlotry. God is unable to live with you as a spiritual harlot. His jealousy in this area would be a godly jealousy. In Ezekiel 8 we read about something that was called the image of Jealousy, and in this case it was the figure of Tammuz. We will read in chapter 8. Then we will go to chapter 16 and talk about spiritual whoredoms. All of this is rooted in Jealousy.

There is another dimension that needs to be broken concerning your release from the judgments against you for fornicating spiritually with false religions and doctrines of devils throughout your entire life and in your ancestral line.

You have to be released from judgments against you for fornicating spiritually with false religions and doctrines of devils so you can be free from the occult.

There has to be a breaking. There has to be a place that you come into with the Lord so that He can trust you as His spiritual wife forever when it comes to spiritual things. He is not going to share you with a mythological entity. He is not going to share you with the devil. He is not going to share you with a false religion. He is not going to share you with divination. He is not going to share you with any of this stuff. He wants the purity of His relationship with you.

Decision and conviction precede freedom.

The fruit of that freedom usually shows up in the near future. Immediate conclusions are not always complete because God is still "working over" your heart and other

71

people's hearts. Do not go by immediate manifestation. In the long term, look for changes. After you notice that the torment is gone, then you will realize there is good fruit.

No longer having the torment you used to have is an indication that the spirit has been removed.

Judge it by the fruit of it.

Ezekiel says,

> ¹And it came to pass in the sixth year, in the sixth *month*, in the fifth *day* of the month, *as* I sat in mine house, and the elders of Judah sat before me, that the hand of the Lord GOD fell there upon me.
> ²Then I beheld, and lo a likeness as the appearance of fire: from the appearance of his loins even downward, fire; and from his loins even upward, as the appearance of brightness, as the colour of amber.
> ³And he put forth the form of an hand, and took me by a lock of mine head; and the spirit lifted me up between the earth and the heaven, and brought me in the visions of God to Jerusalem, to the door of the inner gate that looketh toward the north; where *was* the seat of the image of jealousy, which provoketh to jealousy.   Ezekiel 8:1-3

In this case, this is not the Jealousy of man over love. This is not about the rage of man in Envy and Jealousy. It's about God's zeal for you, His people. He is not going to share you with the devil. *He is not going to share you.* Do you think God should share you with the devil or a false religion? Do you think He has a zeal toward you? He wants your integrity before Him to be pure. The image of Jealousy was Tammuz. It was a symbol of idolatry. These were not the pagans in Ezekiel 8. This was the Old Testament church, the Jews, and they were coming to the temple, God's place of worship, to worship a different husband.

The Scriptures are filled with examples of the Lord being your spiritual husband forever. You are betrothed eternally to the Lord Jesus as your spiritual husband, whether you are male or female, single or married. This is not in the carnal sense of sexuality, but in the mystical sense of union as a help meet, as the one you look to, your *Adon*, your spiritual head, your spiritual leader whom you will follow. It is difficult for a man to understand, but Jesus is my husband too. Because I understand it spiritually, it causes and allows me to be a better husband on earth. Because I understand who my spiritual husband is, I have a good pattern as a husband on earth. If you want to be a good wife, then see what the Lord wants for you in the church, and you will be a good wife. Both husbands and wives naturally need to get a revelation of what relationship is all about.

In the tribulation period while the antichrist is besieging the Jews, you will be in heaven, first of all, for the judgment seat of Christ and second, for the marriage supper of the Lamb in which your spiritual husband will be wedded to you and you to Him forever as His help meet. The groom is Jesus. You and I are the bride and mystically, forever we shall be united with Him. Both male and female, Old and New Testament saints, everyone who has been redeemed, who has been in covenant, who has responded to the Spirit of God, will also be known as the bride of the groom.

So here is the Lord looking down on His betrothed wife. In Jewish custom, if you are betrothed, the same requirements that applied to the marriage applied to betrothal. That is what happened to Joseph and Mary over the virgin birth of Christ. She was found to be with child; she was betrothed to him, and it would have been adultery. Whether or not the marriage had been consummated, in the Jewish way of thinking, which was God's way of thinking, the betrothal was the same thing as marriage.

So here is God looking down from heaven. He has taken Ezekiel up into a vision in which he is looking down on God's people and guess who is in the door of the temple? The image of Jealousy. This is a type of spiritual harlotry. If I have any fear from a godly standpoint, my greatest fear as a Christian, my greatest fear as a man, is to be deceived by error. My greatest fear is deception and divination.

I cannot afford to follow a lie.

I cannot afford or allow anything to come into my thinking that would not match these scriptures because that would be spiritual harlotry. I cannot fathom serving another god. It is contrary to my very nature. It is contrary to my heart, yet those gods sometimes are very insidious, aren't they? Those gods will come into our lives, and the first thing you know, we are having a little time of fellowship with them until finally we find ourselves in a whale of a mess.

In Ezekiel 8, the image of Jealousy which provokes to Jealousy was an idol of a mythological god the pagan nations worshipped. That was not as much of a concern to God as His own wife worshipping another god; that meant she had a different husband. In order to understand the spiritual significance, we had to go to the natural first. We could not go to the spiritual first because we had some things to resolve before the Lord in our lives. Now we are coming over here to the spiritual level looking at Him and saying, "Yes, Lord, I may have done things in my life; I was unfaithful to you spiritually. I may have followed this and I may have followed that. I may have gone here and I may have gone there. I was unfaithful to you. I whored around on You, God, and I am a spiritual harlot.

The greatest love story ever told is that God eternally married a harlot. I do not know about you, but I was a spiritual whore. I knew I was separated from Him. I knew I was a sinner, because I had violated the covenant. Now being restored to Him in that relationship is the most important thing in my life. I do not want to become separated from my husband ever again. That does not mean

I don't have my days, but He is a faithful husband. The church, His wife, and the world today are pretty close together. We have the same glitches. Well, I thank God that the Lord, as a husband, is a little different than most husbands in the world today. He is perfect. Men, we can take a good lesson from Him.

> ⁴And, behold, the glory of the God of Israel *was* there, according to the vision that I saw in the plain.
>
> ⁵Then said he unto me, Son of man, lift up thine eyes now the way toward the north. So I lifted up mine eyes the way toward the north, and behold northward at the gate of the altar this image of jealousy in the entry.
>
> ⁶He said furthermore unto me, Son of man, seest thou what they do? *even* the great abominations that the house of Israel committeth here, that I should go far off from my sanctuary? but turn thee yet again, *and* thou shalt see greater abominations.
>
> ⁷And he brought me to the door of the court; and when I looked, behold a hole in the wall.
>
> ⁸Then said he unto me, Son of man, dig now in the wall: and when I had digged in the wall, behold a door.
>
> ⁹And he said unto me, Go in, and behold the wicked abominations that they do here.   Ezekiel 8:4-9

Who was doing it? God's people.

Where? In the sanctuary.

> ¹⁰So I went in and saw; and behold every form of creeping things, and abominable beasts, and all the idols of the house of Israel, portrayed upon the wall round about.
>
> ¹¹And there stood before them seventy men of the ancients of the house of Israel...   Ezekiel 8:10-11

These are the leaders.

> ¹¹...and in the midst of them stood Jaazaniah the son of Shaphan, with every man his censer in his hand; and a thick cloud of incense went up.
>
> ¹²Then said he unto me, Son of man, hast thou seen what the ancients of the house of Israel do in the dark, every man in the

chambers of his imagery? for they say, The LORD seeth us not; the LORD hath forsaken the earth.

¹³He said also unto me, Turn thee yet again, *and* thou shalt see greater abominations that they do.

¹⁴Then he brought me to the door of the gate of the LORD's house which *was* toward the north; and, behold, there sat women weeping for Tammuz.

¹⁵Then said he unto me, Hast thou seen *this*, O son of man? turn thee yet again, *and* thou shalt see greater abominations than these.

¹⁶And he brought me into the inner court of the LORD's house, and, behold, at the door of the temple of the LORD, between the porch and the altar, *were* about five and twenty men, with their backs toward the temple of the LORD, and their faces toward the east; and they worshipped the sun toward the east.   Ezekiel 8:11-16

They were worshipping what we know today as eastern mysticism, which is harlotry. Getting direction from where the sun rises is the harlotry. They had their backs toward the temple where the presence of God was supposed to be, and they were literally worshipping the sun. Who else worshipped Ra, the sun god? The Egyptians. The ancient god of the Egyptians was Ra, the sun god. When you see these big circles with the little fire things going around, that is Ra. That imagery is the image of Ra, coming out of Egyptian mythology. To wear that stuff as jewelry is to exalt the sun god Ra. In Jacksonville, Florida there is a large Masonic Temple, and up in the very corner it says Ra. There is a picture of the sun, because they are worshipping the sun god Ra of Egyptian mythology.

¹⁷Then he said unto me, Hast thou seen *this*, O son of man? Is it a light thing to the house of Judah that they commit the abominations which they commit here? for they have filled the land with violence, and have returned to provoke me to anger: and, lo, they put the branch to their nose.

¹⁸Therefore will I also deal in fury: mine eye shall not spare, neither will I have pity: and though they cry in mine ears with a loud voice, *yet* will I not hear them.   Ezekiel 8:17-18

This is a parallel of the evil part of Jealousy and is an area in which God is not going to share you with another. I have news for those who are born again, yet say you can live like the devil and go to heaven, while preaching eternal security. You are eternal and secure as long as you stay eternally secure in the Father through Jesus Christ. Freedom without responsibility is dangerous. I do not preach legalism. I do not preach bondage. I do not put people in a straight jacket, but I do teach this: that with freedom comes great responsibility. Even in America, our freedom requires great responsibility. *You cannot have your freedom and live an unrighteous lifestyle.*

Ezekiel 16 is an incredibly powerful, incredibly beautiful chapter. It is really the story of the birth and the coming to maturity of the son or daughter of God.

> ¹Again the word of the LORD came unto me, saying,
>
> ²Son of man, cause Jerusalem to know her abominations,
>
> ³And say, Thus saith the Lord GOD unto Jerusalem; Thy birth and thy nativity *is* of the land of Canaan; thy father *was* an Amorite, and thy mother an Hittite.
>
> ⁴And *as for* thy nativity, in the day thou wast born thy navel was not cut, neither wast thou washed in water to supple *thee;* thou wast not salted at all, nor swaddled at all.
>
> ⁵None eye pitied thee, to do any of these unto thee, to have compassion upon thee; but thou wast cast out in the open field, to the lothing of thy person, in the day that thou wast born.
>
> ⁶And when I passed by thee, and saw thee polluted in thine own blood, I said unto thee *when thou wast* in thy blood, Live; yea, I said unto thee *when thou wast* in thy blood, Live.
>
> Ezekiel 16:1-6

God is saying is that you were born, rejected, and trashed by the very acts of sin. You were polluted in your own blood. You were born out of sin. The Hittite and the Amorite represent the pagan nations. God was saying that on the day you were born, you were rejected. Many of us were rejected at birth or were rejected in the womb and not wanted. The Lord is saying, "Listen, I passed by. I saw you lying there dying in your own birth blood. No one swaddled you; no one took care of you. I passed by and said, I want that one. Live!" God is saying, "I picked you up and I nurtured you. I raised you and I took you for my own out of your death, out of your disease, out of your Rejection, out of your abandonment, and for all I did, you turned into a whore as a thank you to me for loving you." This is tough talk, but it is true talk, and it is right here in the Word.

Then you developed into your womanhood and I caused you to multiply as a bud of the field, and you have increased and waxen greatly. You have come to excellent ornaments. Your breasts are fashioned and your hair is grown whereas you were naked and bare.

> I have caused thee to multiply as the bud of the field, and thou hast increased and waxen great, and thou art come to excellent ornaments: *thy* breasts are fashioned, and thine hair is grown, whereas thou *wast* naked and bare.　　　Ezekiel 16:7

In other words, He has nurtured you and brought you up to your place of maturity. You have come through your puberty. You have come into your womanhood, and you have come into that place of beauty. Whereas before, you were naked and bare, now you are fashioned and fully furnished in all dimensions, including the physical.

> [8]Now when I passed by thee, and looked upon thee, behold, thy time *was* the time of love; and I spread my skirt over thee, and covered thy nakedness: yea, I sware unto thee, and entered into a covenant with thee, saith the Lord GOD, and thou becamest mine.
>
> [9]Then washed I thee with water; yea, I throughly washed away thy blood from thee, and I anointed thee with oil.
>
> [10]I clothed thee also with broidered work, and shod thee with badgers' skin, and I girded thee about with fine linen, and I covered thee with silk.
>
> [11]I decked thee also with ornaments, and I put bracelets upon thy hands, and a chain on thy neck.
>
> [12]And I put a jewel on thy forehead, and earrings in thine ears, and a beautiful crown upon thine head.

¹³Thus wast thou decked with gold and silver; and thy raiment *was of* fine linen, and silk, and broidered work; thou didst eat fine flour, and honey, and oil: and thou wast exceeding beautiful, and thou didst prosper into a kingdom.

¹⁴And thy renown went forth among the heathen for thy beauty: for it *was* perfect through my comeliness, which I had put upon thee, saith the Lord GOD.

¹⁵But thou didst trust in thine own beauty, and playedst the harlot because of thy renown, and pouredst out thy fornications on every one that passed by; his it was.

¹⁶And of thy garments thou didst take, and deckedst thy high places with divers colours, and playedst the harlot thereupon: *the like things* shall not come, neither shall it be so.

¹⁷Thou hast also taken thy fair jewels of my gold and of my silver, which I had given thee, and madest to thyself images of men, and didst commit whoredom with them.

Ezekiel 16:8-17

This would be Tammuz.

You had all the beauty, all the gold, all the splendor, all the blessings, all the help and all the places of preeminence as a nation and a people. Yet as a nation and as a people of God, you took my blessing and fashioned it into idolatry.

¹⁸And tookest thy broidered garments, and coveredst them: and thou hast set mine oil and mine incense before them.

¹⁹My meat also which I gave thee, fine flour, and oil, and honey, wherewith I fed thee, thou hast even set it before them for a sweet savour: and thus it was, saith the Lord God.

²⁰Moreover thou hast taken thy sons and thy daughters, whom thou hast borne unto me, and these hast thou sacrificed unto them to be devoured. Is this of thy whoredoms a small matter,

²¹That thou hast slain my children, and delivered them to cause them to pass through the fire for them? Ezekiel 16:18-21

This is where they would actually throw the children and the babies into the fire to be burned as a sacrifice to the god Molech. These were the very children that God gave them to be given back to Himself in their generations, and they sacrificed them to devils.

²²And in all thine abominations and thy whoredoms thou hast not remembered the days of thy youth, when thou wast naked and bare, *and* wast polluted in thy blood.

²³And it came to pass after all thy wickedness, (woe, woe unto thee! saith the Lord GOD;)

²⁴*That* thou hast also built unto thee an eminent place, and hast made thee an high place in every street.

²⁵Thou hast built thy high place at every head of the way, and hast made thy beauty to be abhorred, and hast opened thy feet to every one that passed by, and multiplied thy whoredoms.

²⁶Thou hast also committed fornication with the Egyptians thy neighbours, great of flesh; and hast increased thy whoredoms, to provoke me to anger.   Ezekiel 16:22-26

How would you commit fornication with the Egyptians? By the worship of the sun god Ra, by the worship of the paganistic cultures and the divinations and all the ideologies and philosophies of pagan nations. You went their way of pagan worship. You worshipped their deities, you worshipped their mythologies, you worshipped the sun, moon and stars. You worshipped animals. You have made cows and beetles and spiders and things of stone and wood your worship deities.

²⁶Thou hast also committed fornication with the Egyptians thy neighbours, great of flesh; and hast increased thy whoredoms, to provoke me to anger.

²⁷Behold, therefore I have stretched out my hand over thee, and have diminished thine ordinary *food,* and delivered thee unto the will of them that hate thee, the daughters of the Philistines, which are ashamed of thy lewd way.

²⁸Thou hast played the whore also with the Assyrians, because thou wast unsatiable; yea, thou hast played the harlot with them, and yet couldest not be satisfied.

²⁹Thou hast moreover multiplied thy fornication in the land of Canaan unto Chaldea; and yet thou wast not satisfied herewith.

³⁰How weak is thine heart, saith the Lord GOD, seeing thou doest all these *things,* the work of an imperious whorish woman;

³¹In that thou buildest thine eminent place in the head of every way, and makest thine high place in every street; and hast not been as an harlot, in that thou scornest hire;

³²*But as* a wife that committeth adultery, *which* taketh strangers instead of her husband!

³³They give gifts to all whores: but thou givest thy gifts to all thy lovers, and hirest them, that they may come unto thee on every side for thy whoredom.

³⁴And the contrary is in thee from *other* women in thy whoredoms, whereas none followeth thee to commit whoredoms: and in that thou givest a reward, and no reward is given unto thee, therefore thou art contrary.

³⁵Wherefore, O harlot, hear the word of the LORD:

³⁶Thus saith the Lord GOD; Because thy filthiness was poured out, and thy nakedness discovered through thy whoredoms with thy lovers, and with all the idols of thy abominations, and by the blood of thy children, which thou didst give unto them;

³⁷Behold, therefore I will gather all thy lovers, with whom thou hast taken pleasure, and all *them* that thou hast loved, with all *them* that thou hast hated; I will even gather them round about against thee, and will discover thy nakedness unto them, that they may see all thy nakedness.

³⁸And I will judge thee, as women that break wedlock and shed blood are judged; and I will give thee blood in fury and jealousy. Ezekiel 16:26-38

Here is the Jealousy.

³⁹And I will also give thee into their hand, and they shall throw down thine eminent place, and shall break down thy high places: they shall strip thee also of thy clothes, and shall take thy fair jewels, and leave thee naked and bare.

⁴⁰They shall also bring up a company against thee, and they shall stone thee with stones, and thrust thee through with their swords.

⁴¹And they shall burn thine houses with fire, and execute judgments upon thee in the sight of many women: and I will cause thee to cease from playing the harlot, and thou also shalt give no hire any more.

⁴²So will I make my fury toward thee to rest, and my jealousy shall depart from thee, and I will be quiet, and will be no more angry.

43Because thou hast not remembered the days of thy youth, but hast fretted me in all these *things*; behold, therefore I also will recompense thy way upon *thine* head, saith the Lord GOD: and thou shalt not commit this lewdness above all thine abominations.

44Behold, every one that useth proverbs shall use *this* proverb against thee, saying, As *is* the mother, *so is* her daughter.

45Thou *art* thy mother's daughter, that lotheth her husband and her children; and thou *art* the sister of thy sisters, which lothed their husbands and their children: your mother *was* an Hittite, and your father an Amorite.

46And thine elder sister *is* Samaria, she and her daughters that dwell at thy left hand: and thy younger sister, that dwelleth at thy right hand, *is* Sodom and her daughters.

47Yet hast thou not walked after their ways, nor done after their abominations: but, as *if that were* a very little *thing*, thou wast corrupted more than they in all thy ways.

48*As* I live, saith the Lord GOD, Sodom thy sister hath not done, she nor her daughters, as thou hast done, thou and thy daughters.

49Behold, this was the iniquity of thy sister Sodom, pride, fulness of bread, and abundance of idleness was in her and in her daughters, neither did she strengthen the hand of the poor and needy.

50And they were haughty, and committed abomination before me: therefore I took them away as I saw *good*.

51Neither hath Samaria committed half of thy sins; but thou hast multiplied thine abominations more than they, and hast justified thy sisters in all thine abominations which thou hast done.

52Thou also, which hast judged thy sisters, bear thine own shame for thy sins that thou hast committed more abominable than they: they are more righteous than thou: yea, be thou confounded also, and bear thy shame, in that thou hast justified thy sisters.

53When I shall bring again their captivity, the captivity of Sodom and her daughters, and the captivity of Samaria and her daughters, then *will I bring again* the captivity of thy captives in the midst of them:

54That thou mayest bear thine own shame, and mayest be confounded in all that thou hast done, in that thou art a comfort unto them.

⁵⁵When thy sisters, Sodom and her daughters, shall return to their former estate, and Samaria and her daughters shall return to their former estate, then thou and thy daughters shall return to your former estate.

⁵⁶For thy sister Sodom was not mentioned by thy mouth in the day of thy pride,

⁵⁷Before thy wickedness was discovered, as at the time of *thy* reproach of the daughters of Syria, and all *that are* round about her, the daughters of the Philistines, which despise thee round about.

⁵⁸Thou hast borne thy lewdness and thine abominations, saith the LORD.

⁵⁹For thus saith the Lord GOD; I will even deal with thee as thou hast done, which hast despised the oath in breaking the covenant. Ezekiel 16:39-59

Verse 60 is of tremendous promise and we are coming into this promise today for our lives.

⁶⁰Nevertheless I will remember my covenant with thee in the days of thy youth, and I will establish unto thee an everlasting covenant.

⁶¹Then thou shalt remember thy ways, and be ashamed, when thou shalt receive thy sisters, thine elder and thy younger: and I will give them unto thee for daughters, but not by thy covenant.

⁶²And I will establish my covenant with thee; and thou shalt know that I *am* the LORD:

⁶³That thou mayest remember, and be confounded, and never open thy mouth any more because of thy shame, when I am pacified toward thee for all that thou hast done, saith the Lord GOD. Ezekiel 16:60-63

By the way, this is *Adonay Yhovih*, the Father, speaking.

We have to get our peace before God in the area of personal relationships, husband or wife, male and female. We have to come and take responsibility for our spiritual whoredom before God in the area of occultism, false religions and error, worshipping gods and devils. We have to go there, not only for your life, but also for your ancestral line. That includes anything your parents have been involved with in paganism. That includes any false religion, any philosophy or ideology that would separate you from the love of God. You know what they are. So pause now and get your peace with God, repent for your generations and for your own personal separation.

PRAYER - *SPIRITUAL WHOREDOMS*

Father God, I thank You for today. Father, we hear the word of the Lord. We were called out of desolation, out of abandonment, out of the pollution of our own blood. You loved us and we thank You for it. In our ancestry, our ancestors have not always fully followed you. They have followed Tammuz. They have followed Ra the sun god. They have worshipped stone. They have worshipped things of the devil. They have worshipped false religions. They have denied the living God. They have not followed the God that made them. They have not followed the God that delivered them. They have not followed the God that loved them, but in their haughtiness, in their pride, they have whored after other gods.

My ancestors have turned away from the truth of the living God, and in my own personal life, I possibly have followed other gods, other philosophies, other religions. I have worshipped other deities. I have worshipped devils. I have been a spiritual whore. My ancestors have been spiritual whores, and we have left our husband. We have left and followed other husbands, but those other husbands turned against us and devastated us. They did not love us. They destroyed us, and in our whoredoms they were not good husbands to us.

Father, thank You for the Lord Jesus. Thank You that Jesus came to save us from our whoredoms. Thank you that He came to save us from the pollution of our blood. Thank you that He came to redeem us from our ancestral curses. Just as Ezekiel said, we are the daughter of our mother, indicating the inherited rollover, the inherited curse of whoredoms, not just for the females, but for the males. In our family tree, male and female, we have erred, we are the sons and daughters of our mothers and fathers, in our whoredoms, in our apostasies, in our ignorance, in our lust, in our pride. We left You, God. Thank You for coming back to get us.

We take responsibility today, Father, before You for all error, all apostasy of thinking, all false doctrine, all false religion. We repent to You for not loving You fully, Father. We repent to You, Lord Jesus, for not loving You fully. It is in our hearts today to be a good wife to You, not out of performance, but because we are in covenant. Not out of requirement, but because that is where our heart is. We are in relationship one with another, and You are a good father and a good husband. We thank You for it. We repent, God, and ask to be delivered today for the inherited curse of whoredoms coming out of our lives today. We know that You are jealous over us Lord, in that You will not share us with another. Lord we ask that You continue to be jealous over us and bless us according to Your heart, not according to the error of our ways. All the people said, Amen.

Take this time to go before the Lord in your generations and your personal life and deal with all religions, all religious spirits, all whoredoms, all chasing this and that, and all of the Tammuzes, the idols of your heart that you have actually worshipped. You have faced them in temples or you have faced them in books, or you have faced them wherever. Repent to God for your spiritual whoredoms so the spirit of Jealousy can be lifted and the Spirit of God can be released to you for benefit and for blessing and that God will remember who He saved. Amen?

I want you to say:

> Father, take away the images of Jealousy from my heart. I am the temple of the Holy Ghost. God, You don't reside in a building; You reside in my spirit as a work of the Holy Spirit.

> I pull down the images of Jealousy from the doorways of my temple. So when You look into my heart, when

> You look into those dark places inside the temple, Father, You are not going to find abominations in there. You are not going to find the idols of Tammuz. You are not going to find me facing and worshipping the sun god. You are not going to see images of creepy, abominable animals on my walls. But you are going to look into my heart, and my heart is going to be looking back at You.

> Take away, God, the images of Jealousy that would provoke, and Lord, let not Your zeal be quenched. Let me respond to Your zeal. Let Your jealousy, which is good, be over me; let me be jealous for You, Lord. Let my zeal and Your zeal mingle together and let our relationship be one. Let the abominations go by the wayside. Let our hearts beat as one, because You said in the Word that You and Jesus are one, and that if we are in Jesus, we

would be one with You, Father. We want that relationship. We want that zeal to be there.

Take not your jealousy from us, but let the image of Jealousy be cast down. Let our zeal be our zeal together. Let's be **HOT** concerning You, God. You said it, Jesus, in the church of Laodicea, "I wish you were cold. I wish you were hot, but because you are lukewarm, I am going to spew you out of my mouth." I want to be **HOT** for You, God. I want to be **HOT** for You as You are **HOT** for me. I do not want any false religions and junk to come into my life. I do not want to get sidetracked. I remember the day of my pollution, and I am a grateful wife.

Thank You for restoring me from my whoredoms. Thank You for loving me while I was still in my whoredoms. Thank You that in the midst of Your jealousy for me, You did not forget me. You came for me and I responded. I thank You for Your zeal concerning me, God. Cast me not away from Your presence. Take not Your Holy Spirit from me, but let me be reunited with You in the purity of union. In the Spirit, in the name of the Lord Jesus Christ, we thank You, Father. Amen.

Is the Lord looking down from heaven into the doorways of your temple to find no image standing, blocking His view? Are you weeping for Tammuz or are you weeping for Him? Your heart needs to be where the Lamb is. Where the Lamb goes, I am going. I am not going to stop and worry about some dead cow. My father owns the cattle on a thousand hills. I am going to follow Him. I am going to get those images out of my heart. I have been a spiritual harlot in my time. I was so darkened at one point in my life that God to me was no more than some type of cosmic awareness. He did not exist; it was just some kind of force that might have been in the universe. That is how far my heart was darkened. That is how far I was from Him. I remember the days of my pollution. I remember the days of my abandonment. I remember the days of my wickedness, and I remember the days of my nakedness. I know what I have been saved from and I know what I have been saved to. I am not going back. I do not want the spirit of Jealousy to come into me, and I do not want the Lord's jealousy to be hot against me in harlotry.

> Father, in the name of the Lord Jesus Christ, according to the integrity of their hearts, I believe they are casting down the images of Jealousy today. They are casting them far from them and they have repented for the idolatry of their ancestry. It does not have to be "like father, like son." It does not have to be "like mother, like daughter." It has to go: like the husband, so goes the wife. That is where we want to go, Father. We want the spiritual understanding of the pursuit of Your heart and what You have done by sending us the Lord Jesus for our hearts. Take those images that were within us, Lord God, those images that would provoke Jealousy to open the doors to our desolation. We thank you for your grace and your mercy, and we release You, Father, not to the image of Jealousy, but in my prayer I ask You, Lord, do not stop being jealous over me in the godly sense. Don't stop being jealous over me; be hot towards me, God. Continue to desire to be in fellowship with me as I continue to desire to be in fellowship with You.

I want to tell you something: God desires your fellowship with Him and desires to walk in the cool of the evening with you every day. God desires your fellowship.

He desires your presence. He wants you to be His best friend. In fact, Jesus said, I no longer call you servants, but I call you friends. Before you can have a relationship in the physical sense, you have to be friends. A marriage does not work unless you are friends. Jesus wants you as a friend. He said, "You are not my servants, you are my friends." That creates a standpoint and a foundation for Him to be your eternal husband forever. Isn't it wonderful to be in love with your first love and your best friend? Understand the depth of relationship, the depth of commitment, the depth of covenant, and the depth of fellowship, so that nothing can separate you at this level. If you aren't careful and something does come to separate you, guess what starts to be built in the doorway of your temple. The image of Jealousy. I do not know about you today, but I am really turned on about God. I really rededicate my heart today before the living God that any images of Jealousy would be taken from my heart.

Envy and Jealousy are destructive forces that will take away your freedom and put you in a place of bondage. Have you made your peace with God in the area of Jealousy from a husband or lover? Have you made your peace with God, the lover of your soul? He loves you with an everlasting love, and He is not going to share you with another. That is a good jealousy, not the destructive, evil Jealousy. It is the powerful, jealous zeal of relationship and the keeping of covenant even in sin. Evil Jealousy destroys forever, but the jealousy of God, even after failure, comes to woo you, to treat you as if you were faithful and to receive your repentance and restore you to a place of intimate fellowship. I am going to be *HOT* for God; how about you?

> Father, thank You for this day. Thank You for giving us the ability to articulate this at this level. It is just almost impossible to be able to articulate the depth of Your heart concerning this issue. I trust we have done the best we can.

For that matter, we did not have to say much because Ezekiel said it all. We thank you, God, that Ezekiel wrote this so that we could learn about the aspects of Jealousy and the zeal of God towards our heart and our ancestral separation from our eternal spiritual husband and our eternal spiritual Father.

CHOICES

The Father wants to give you away to your husband, Jesus. You have been created at the will of the Father for the Lord Jesus Christ, who is your Creator from the beginning, and you are a gift of God to Jesus Christ. But do you know what Jesus does with you? He gives you back to the Father, and the Father gives you back to Him. What a wonderful, wonderful place to be, to have a husband and a Father at that level, eternally. Because you have experienced His forgiveness, because you have experienced His love, and because you understand the covenant nature of what we are discussing, you will have an assignment as kings and priests beginning in the millennium and on into the new heavens and the new earth. Do you know what you are going to get a chance to do? You will teach natural man the dynamics of the depth of this type of *HOT* relationship with each other and with God. You get a chance to practice it here right now, to understand it here right now, and you get a chance to make it part of your life right now. O taste and see that the Lord, He is good.

> **O taste and see that the LORD *is* good: blessed *is* the man *that* trusteth in him.** Psalms 34:8

When you come before God, Envy and Jealousy start pecking at your back door. You first must make a quality decision that you are not going to have it as part of your life. You can resist it all you want, but if you love it, it is not going anywhere. You may not like the fruit of it, you may not like the passion of it, you may not like what it is doing, but you are going to have to get something straight.

Unless you have a perfect hatred for Envy and Jealousy, you cannot ever be delivered from it.

Ezekiel says,

> Therefore, as I live, saith the Lord GOD, I will even do according to thine anger, and according to thine envy which thou hast used out of thy hatred against them; and I will make myself known among them, when I have judged thee.
>
> **Ezekiel 35:11**

What you sow, you are going to reap. If you sow unto Envy and Jealousy, you are going to reap the rewards of Envy and Jealousy. If you sow unto hatred, what are you going to reap? If you sow unto Bitterness, what are you going to reap?

The Word says in Matthew that those sins which you retain in another are retained, and those sins that you remit in another are remitted.

> Whose soever sins ye remit, they are remitted unto them; *and* whose soever *sins* ye retain, they are retained.   John 20:23

When you retain something against a person, it is retained. Whatever you bind in earth is bound in heaven. Whatever you loose in earth is loosed in heaven. That has nothing to do with prosperity. That has to do with relationship coming out of Bitterness and forgiveness. Matthew 18 has to do with forgiveness. So if you want to bind Bitterness in the earth, do you know how you can do it and bind it in heaven for you? Just keep living it.

Bind Bitterness in heaven and earth.

When you don't release that anger, when you don't release that retaliation, when you don't release that resentment, when you don't release that Envy, when you don't release that Jealousy against people, then you are binding it as a force in the earth in them <u>and in you</u>. When you release them and forgive them, you release them and you release yourself.

In understanding the Godhead revelation in Ezekiel 35:11, the Father is speaking. This is *Adonay Yhovih*, Lord GOD. *Adonay Yhovih*, the Father. He is saying that if this is the lifestyle you are choosing and it is evil, this is the lifestyle that you shall be judged by. You are going to reap what you sow. A Beatitude in Matthew says,

> **Blessed *are* the merciful: for they shall obtain mercy.**
> **Matthew 5:7**

How do you get mercy? You give it. Choose this day what you shall have, blessings or cursings, life or death.

> **I call heaven and earth to record this day against you, *that* I have set before you life and death, blessing and cursing: therefore choose life, that both thou and thy seed may live:**
> **Deuteronomy 30:19**

If you come for ministry and have Bitterness, then you have the consequences of Bitterness in your life in disease. If you come with Envy and Jealousy, and you have rottenness in your bones and the consequences of the curse within you, or if you come with Jealousy between a husband and wife and you have gastrointestinal problems and a rotten thigh, if you do not deal with these roots, then you are going to keep the diseases. You are going to keep the torment, and you are going to keep the diseases you have because God is not going to heal you.

I don't care how much spiritual warfare you do. I don't care how many scriptures you confess. I don't care how many scripture keys that you try to memorize. There is an *if,* a *then,* and a *but* you must deal with and that is your choice. You can jump up and down on the Bible. You can pray, you can fast, you can scream, you can beg, you can cry, and you can do what you want. Until you deal with the spiritual dynamics, God's ears are deaf unto you. He will give to you the very thing that you are sowing unto mankind yourself; He will let you reap of that. That is the bottom line.

Ezekiel says I will do to you according to your anger, I will do to you according to your Envy, and I will do to you according to your Bitterness and your hatred. If you want to sow that garbage from hell, then do not cry unto me because you are reaping the fruit of it. There is a balance in all of this. You ask, "What is the use of crying to God if He is not going to listen and is not going to hear?" But He will.

CONDITIONS FOR GOD HEARING YOU

There are conditions for God hearing you. If you're crying out to God because you're devastated by this stuff, and you just want to be free because you are tired of the devastation, He isn't going to hear you. But if you cry out unto God because you are convicted, because you understand why you are all goofed up with this stuff and because you have a repentant heart, then He is going to deliver you.

Cry out to God because you are convicted!

But He is not going to deliver you and free you and let you continue to live your life with this stuff still inside your spirit. Why? Because if He delivers you from the diseases, both psychological and biological, and if the torment that has occurred is because you have this in your life, then guess what is still there? The Bitterness and the Envy and the Jealousy and the same old fruit. God is wasting His time delivering you of a disease and an oppression if He lets the spiritual dynamics that are producing it stay within you.

Why would you come if you don't expect to get rid of it? I can see you going to a dentist now. "Oh dentist, I have a cavity." "Well let me fix it." "No, sorry. I just wanted you to see I had a cavity." "Let me see. Sure enough. I can help you." "No, I don't want help. I just need a confirmation."

A lot of people are spectators. We don't want spectators. We want people to get rid of their junk. If you don't deal with these things, they're going to deal with you. One thing I learned about the scriptures from the Old Testament is that when any of God's people cohabited with an enemy and didn't destroy it, that enemy came back to haunt them the rest of their days.

Anything you agree with and allow to stay in your turf has the right to your life.

Anything you agree with can stay in your life!

That's a very powerful axiom of truth I'm giving you. Whatever you allow, you allow. Whatever you disallow, you disallow. Choose this day what you shall have – blessings or cursings, life or death.

It's a quality decision. Salvation is a quality decision. Why don't you make a quality decision that you don't want this junk, this plaque of hell, attached to your spiritual life? Amen?

You have to make up your mind that you don't want it.

So what is my job with you? To teach you truth according to 2 Timothy 2 so that you may repent. That God peradventure... I love that term, peradventure. It's almost like a slot machine - you wonder what's coming out next.

That God, peradventure, will give you repentance to the acknowledging of the truth that you may recover yourself from the snare of the devil. God wants to heal you. God wants to save you. God wants to deliver you, but He doesn't want to do it at the expense of you not participating with Him forever in that freedom. Why? Because now you can teach others the error of their ways.

> 24And the servant of the Lord must not strive; but be gentle unto all *men*, apt to teach, patient,
> 25In meekness instructing those that oppose themselves; if God peradventure will give them repentance to the acknowledging of the truth;
> 26And *that* they may recover themselves out of the snare of the devil, who are taken captive by him at his will.
> 2 Timothy 2:24-26

What did David say in Psalm 51? What did David say about the area of adultery and what he did to Uriah the

Hittite, in having him killed? The Bible says David was perfect in all his ways as a man, except in the matter of Uriah the Hittite. Psalm 51 is the greatest prayer of salvation in the entire Bible. David is repenting in verse 3 because he is a man who was caught in sin.

David said,

> ³For I acknowledge my transgressions: and my sin *is* ever before me.
> ⁷Purge me with hyssop, and I shall be clean: wash me, and I shall be whiter than snow.
> ⁸Make me to hear joy and gladness; *that* the bones *which* thou hast broken may rejoice.
> ⁹Hide thy face from my sins, and blot out all mine iniquities.
> ¹⁰Create in me a clean heart, O God; and renew a right spirit within me.
> ¹¹Cast me not away from thy presence; and take not thy holy spirit from me.
> ¹²Restore unto me the joy of thy salvation; and uphold me *with thy* free spirit. Psalm 51:3, 7-12

FRUIT OF THE ROOT

God wants to deliver you of the root problem that is causing the bigger problem, which is the fruit of the root.

**You are so busy wanting to be free of the
<u>fruit of the root</u>
that you forgot to deal with the <u>root</u>.**

You cannot get good fruit and have a bad root. You cannot be free... I don't care how many prayers you say. I don't care how many Bible verses you memorize. I don't care what kind of hype or mantras or meditations you are trying to use to manipulate God.

**You are not going to have good fruit
if you keep the bad root.**

David is saying to God, "Deal with the bad root. Get that thing out of me that is causing the lust and the adultery." When you have been delivered of the bad root, whether it is Bitterness or Envy or Jealousy or whatever it is, you know what you have been delivered from. If you have been healed of that disease in your body, which was the fruit of the root, then you no longer are going to have the disease because the root is gone too. When the root is gone, you do not have any bad fruit. If it was a bad root, then you do not have to worry about it growing again. But if any vestige of that root is left, it can germinate, it can sprout, and it can grow all over again.

We are replacing Bitterness with love, so it's not like there is no fruit. You don't want to be empty and not bear any kind of fruit; plant something in there to replace it!

What good is it to heal you of a disease and let you keep the bad root that is causing the disease? When you have been delivered of Bitterness, Envy and Jealousy, which were paid for at the cross, when you have come before the Father, when you have had a perfect hatred for these things and removed them from your life, when God has delivered you of them, delivered you of the torment, and delivered you of the diseases that have come because of them, then in that day, you can do verse 13. *Then* will I teach transgressors Thy way and sinners can be converted unto Thee. David said, "I am going to teach transgressors *after* I have dealt with my own life, *after* I have dealt with my own bad roots. That wicked thing that is within me has to go. Then can I teach a gospel that will be anointed with power to deliver and to save."

> *Then* will I teach transgressors thy ways; and sinners shall be converted unto thee.   Psalm 51:13

The church today is offering a gospel without responsibility. We are not taking responsibility for sin. We want the blessings, and we are taught the blessings, but...

Blessings come
when we take responsibility for sin.

It's the doctrine of Balaam which says that it is possible. *If, then,* and *but* are conditional to your obedience.

If, Then, and But...

Some people will say that teaching obedience is legalism. No, obedience is not legalism. To "not teach" obedience is to "teach" rebellion and witchcraft. To "not teach" obedience is to "teach" stubbornness and idolatry. Samuel said obedience is better than sacrifice.

> ...Behold, to obey *is* better than sacrifice, *and* to hearken than the fat of rams.   1 Samuel 15:22

PERSONAL RESPONSIBILITY

Responsibility must be taken. In Romans 1, they did not want to retain God in their knowledge so He gave them over to a reprobate mind. They meditated, brooding on evil things; they were full of envy, murder, debate, deceit, malignity, whisperers, backbiters, haters of God, despiteful, proud, boasters, inventors of evil things, disobedient to parents, without understanding, covenant breakers, without natural affection, implacable, unmerciful.

> [28] And even as they did not like to retain God in *their* knowledge, God gave them over to a reprobate mind, to do those things which are not convenient;
> [29] Being filled with all unrighteousness, fornication, wickedness, covetousness, maliciousness; full of envy, murder, debate, deceit, malignity; whisperers,
> [30] Backbiters, haters of God, despiteful, proud, boasters, inventors of evil things, disobedient to parents, [31] Without understanding, covenantbreakers, without natural affection, implacable, unmerciful: Romans 1:28-31

Have you ever seen any of these things hanging around the edges of some humans? Is any of this stuff hanging off you like a dangling participle? It needs to go.

Look at Philippians.

> [15] Some indeed preach Christ even of envy and strife; and some also of good will:
> [16] The one preach Christ of contention, not sincerely, supposing to add affliction to my bonds: Philippians 1:15-16

Some people are argumentative over the Word. They just want to debate it. Some indeed preach Christ even of Envy and strife. Do you know how much competition there is in the body? It's no different in the corporate world. It's no different in the family world, and it's no different in the church. Have you said, "I don't want to be part of the church because I see evil there"? Do you want to see more evil? Then go back into the world. Which is the lesser of the two evils: a sinful church or a sinful world? A sinful world is worse than a sinful church because in the sinful world there is no hope. In a sinful church there is always a chance of change. Christ came to make it possible for us to have a right spirit in spite of sin and to have spiritual understanding and spiritual discernment. Some indeed preach Christ even of Envy and strife.

First Timothy says, "Let as many servants as are under the yoke count their own masters worthy of all honor." By the way, in the context of this, if we went to other scriptures, we could teach you for a long time on the responsibilities of employees to employers. In the historic context of the civilization of that day, if you worked for someone, then he was your master and you were his slave. It was not in terms of free man or bond man, it was in terms of order. Your employer was called a master, and you were his servant. Today we call them employer, employee. Back then it was called master, servant.

> ¹Let as many servants as are under the yoke count their own masters worthy of all honour, that the name of God and *his* doctrine be not blasphemed.
> ²And they that have believing masters, let them not despise *them,* because they are brethren; but rather do *them* service, because they are faithful and beloved, partakers of the benefit. These things teach and exhort.   1 Timothy 6:1-2

As many servants as are under the yoke count their own masters worthy of all honor in order that the name of God and His doctrine be not blasphemed. They that have believing masters, or believing employers, let them not despise them because they are brethren, but rather do them service because they are faithful and beloved.

When I ran businesses before, the worst thing I could do is hire a brother in the Lord because he lost his respect and went into commonness and then broke the godly order. "Oh, you are my brother, now I can do what I want. You can't tell me what to do. Besides, I sit next to you in church on Sundays. You have to let me off the hook. Now those heathen pagans that are working for you, you keep them under your finger." The heathen are more respectful than the brethren. That is an honest but hard-to-hear true statement. Why? Because there is a spirit that comes of Envy and Jealousy and Covetousness and contempt. It is a Luciferian spirit of rebellion.

The Word of God is there to challenge you in your thinking and discernment and to give you some checks and balances. Don't have contempt for your brother and your sister because you are redeemed by the grace of God. If there be one over you in leadership, whether it be in business or ministry, your service, whether in business or in a ministry, is unto the Lord. When you have contempt for your boss or the head over you in ministry, you have contempt for the Lord.

Jesus said very clearly in John, that if they did not receive Him, they did not receive the Father.

He that hateth me hateth my Father also. John 15:23

He also said something else to those of us going out in His name. If they do not receive you when you go out, they have not received Me, and if they have not received Me, they have not received the Father.

Verily, verily, I say unto you, He that receiveth whomsoever I send receiveth me; and he that receiveth me receiveth him that sent me. John 13:20

When someone comes to you as a spiritual leader, you have to make up your mind if that person is or is not a leader to you. If you have any doubt as to his soundness of doctrine and the integrity of his heart, you need to get out because that is leaven to your spirit. Go find someone else to teach you that you respect. You cannot judge one in doctrine when you have not heard it. You have to have your confidence. If you do not have respect for the boss you are working for, then have respect for the Lord. The Lord can judge both your spiritual leader and your boss.

> **If any man teach otherwise, and consent not to wholesome words, *even* the words of our Lord Jesus Christ, and to the doctrine which is according to godliness;** 1 Timothy 6:3

"The doctrine that is according to godliness" — we do not teach legalism. We teach discernment. We do not teach the law. We teach discernment that comes from the law. Legalism is a list of *do and don'ts* simply because they are *do and don'ts;* they have nothing to do with the heart. Legalism is where people are commanded to do things because it is written or said or on a list of *do and don'ts.* That is the law; that is legalism. Legalism is bringing people into a place where you can force them to do something against their wills.

If you want to sin, it's your business. There is a godly order; otherwise we would have anarchy and confusion. No one is allowed to go around and be an island unto themselves; that would be crazy. However, whether you eat pork or you don't eat pork is your business, but don't force it on someone else. To do so would make you legalistic and bring you into legalism. If you do not want to eat pork and that's your conscience, then to eat pork would be a sin unto you.

> **And he that doubteth is damned if he eat, because *he eateth* not of faith: for whatsoever *is* not of faith is sin.** Romans 14:23

If you eat pork, and it's sanctified by the Word of God and by prayer, then eat in moderation. If it is against your conscience, do "not eat" it at all. Because it is against your conscience, do not force someone else to not eat it because that would be legalism.

104

If the person wants to strive, be argumentative and not count his master or his spiritual leader or his employer worthy, he is proud knowing nothing.

> He is proud, knowing nothing, but doting about questions and strifes of words, whereof cometh envy, strife, railings, evil surmisings,   1 Timothy 6:4

When people want to come in strife, and they want to argue about nothing, I recognize that I have ignorance talking to me because they don't know what they're talking about. Yet they are coming across as if they were the great oracle and the great standard of truth in this matter when they do not have the foggiest idea what is going on. That is pride. Paul says that person is proud, knowing nothing, but doting about questions and strifes of words, which is debating, being argumentative. Do not get into strife over the Word.

We all see through a glass darkly and we are all learning every day.

> For now we see through a glass, darkly; but then face to face: now I know in part; but then shall I know even a s also I am known.   1 Corinthians 13:12

No one has all the answers from the Word. When I don't have answers from the Word, I am honest enough to admit it and do a Bible study to find out if God will teach me something. When I have it, I teach it. I do not teach anything that I have not investigated first and understood the context of revealed truth in the Old and New Testaments. I teach only what I have found in context. When I think I have found truth, I go looking for it. When I think I have a new revelation, I am not convinced. When I find truth, I try to prove it wrong first, not right. I want to make sure it is so. I want to make sure there are no missing gaps in it. I want to make sure that when I see it and teach it, people do not receive it just because I teach it. They should receive it because they can see it. They can teach it themselves, and they have the Word to stand on. If you cannot find it for yourself, how can you teach it to anyone?

When I find truth, I go looking for it. If I find a truth in the Word that seems to be right, I go looking for it somewhere else in the Word. When I find it somewhere else and it says the same thing and confirms what I read the first time, I consider that to be confirmation from a scripture verifying a scripture, in context. Then I do a word study to make sure. I find scripture that verifies scripture and that matches another scripture. In the mouth of two or more witnesses, let the Word be established. There are quotations in the New Testament about the Old Testament by different people. Jesus quotes the Old Testament. That is quite a confirmation. If Jesus quoted the Old Testament and made it applicable to the New Covenant, maybe we need to read the Old Testament and see why.

Those of you who think you do not need the Old Testament, you have bought into some divination that is dangerous to your health. Divination is the false voice of the Holy Spirit; it is an evil spirit that counterfeits the Holy Spirit. It can come and bring just as much reality to a person as if it were the Holy Spirit, because it is very spiritual.

Divination is a very dangerous spirit.

In ancient mythologies and Greek mythologies it was called Python. In yoga and eastern mysticism it is called Kundalini. In English, it is called divination. It is an evil spirit that comes to counterfeit the real thing as an oracle of God. But it is not an oracle of God, it is an oracle of the devil.

When Satan came to Eve, he came in divination. When Satan came to Jesus in temptation, he came in divination. When Satan entered into Judas' heart, he came in divination. When Satan entered into Peter's heart, he came in divination. All false prophets are diviners just as much as any fortuneteller. There are people who prophesy in the name of the Lord that are straight from hell, and it is not the Holy Spirit prophesying through them at all; it is a spirit of divination, a counterfeit. How can you tell when it is of God and when it is not of God? It is by the grace of God that you are protected from it.

Again, 1 Timothy says this man is...

> [4]He is proud, knowing nothing, but doting about questions and strifes of words, whereof cometh envy, strife, railings, evil surmisings,
> [5]Perverse disputings of men of corrupt minds, and destitute of the truth, supposing that gain is godliness: from such withdraw thyself.
> [6]But godliness with contentment is great gain.
>
> [7]For we brought nothing into this world, and it is certain we can carry nothing out.
> [8]And having food and raiment let us be therewith content.
> 1 Timothy 6:4-8

Let me help you understand divination because the church is filled with it. It is called seed faith giving and is tied into "name-it-and-claim-it." Divination comes and offers blessings of God just by appropriation, without responsibility. When you say that gain is godliness, you are saying that God's approval on your life is how successful you are, what kind of car you drive, what kind of house you live in, what your bank account is like. These things are not proof of God's blessing on you; that is divination. To teach that gain is godliness is divination.

Do you know how many teach that gain is godliness in the Christian church today?

Divination says gain is godliness.

In some churches you cannot be a leader unless you are successful. In some churches you cannot even be a leader unless you have initials behind your name. Is that truth or error? In some churches you cannot preach the gospel unless you are licensed by that denomination, unless you have a degree from certain seminaries. Is that truth or error? How do I know it is error?

The Bible says this about the apostles: the religious leaders perceived these were unlearned and ignorant men that were turning the world upside down.

> **Now when they saw the boldness of Peter and John, and perceived that they were unlearned and ignorant men, they marvelled; and they took knowledge of them, that they had been with Jesus.** Acts 4:13

Concerning those who are teaching error, Paul says to withdraw yourself from them. But here the Spirit of God says that godliness with contentment is great gain. That is having your peace. Seek ye first the kingdom of God and His righteousness and all these things shall be added unto you.

> **But seek ye first the kingdom of God, and his righteousness; and all these things shall be added unto you.** Matthew 6:33

What comes *first*? The kingdom of God and His righteousness and *then* blessings come. What this is saying is that you seek the kingdom of God first, and then you get the contentment because you have been blessed of God.

3 John 2 is very clear: dearly beloved, I wish above all things that you prosper and be in good health even as your soul prospereth.

> **Beloved, I wish above all things that thou mayest prosper and be in health, even as thy soul prospereth.** 3 John 1:2

The blessings of God in the Old Testament and the New Testament are very evident. There is nothing wrong with being blessed; there is nothing wrong with having a nice car, a nice house, a large bank account, a big business. The issue is the spirit behind it. Is the spirit behind it correct or incorrect? Paul is saying that in the Christian church, leaders must not teach divination to thrust their people into a slot machine mentality — put a nickel in, get a "goody bar" out. We must first seek God's righteousness, His holiness, and His godliness in our life, and *then* there comes the flow of the blessings.

There are many instances of the devil blessing people.

In the blessing, people do not seek God. Our enemy is very shrewd. As an observer of mankind, the worst thing that can happen to some people is for them to make money and to be successful because there is a spiritual problem in them that will turn them away from God. Paul is dealing with the root problem, which is to consider who we are as godly people <u>first</u>. We need to let the blessings stand to the side, and let them be from God.

Prosperity is scriptural, but prosperity comes with a balance of responsibility. Now there is the difference. Maybe we have been so busy promising our people blessings to get them to come out of the world, we forgot to teach righteousness. Seek ye first the kingdom of God and His righteousness. Maybe our people have been taught to lust by our leaders. Maybe our leaders have taught our people to be in Covetousness, or maybe our leaders have taught us to be in Envy and Jealousy because they promote something that cannot be had apart from righteousness, if it comes from God. So the people are being offered blessings, but they do not have to deal with the curses.

You will not get the blessings until you remove the curses.

But the leaders say, "Well, I am sorry, it was a finished thing at the cross. Blessings belong to me now." "Really? Then why do I see curses in your life? If you are free, why do I see the evidence of curses in your life?" No one has ever been able to answer that question for me. That takes the stand that when you are born again, you are free of the curse. I simply look at them and say, "Name me five things that are wrong in your life." They give me the five things. I say, "Deuteronomy 28 says that all of these things are a curse. Then why are you cursed, saint? How can you be free and still be cursed?" No one has been able to answer that question.

Because of what Christ did, now we are free to appropriate what He did for us out of our obedience. It is a beginning. Your spirit comes alive to God and the work of the Holy Spirit in sanctification begins. In some churches you have to be careful because they will not teach sanctification. They will just teach you that now you are the righteousness of God through Christ Jesus, and it is all finished. They teach that you are free, and you just need to believe for your blessings. Well, you are going to get your blessings, but you will not get them if you do not take responsibility for sanctification.

RELATIONSHIP WITH GOD

God is not a slot machine; you don't put money in and get something out. God is a relationship. Your Father loves to bless His children, but it's difficult to bless a child in his sinful ways. If you are a parent, is it is easy to automatically roll over and bless one of your children when he has just been in massive rebellion? Or do you think there needs to be a cooling off time and a place of restriction and reflection? Your Father in heaven is not much different. Would you expect Him to be? As parents, we are always looking for ways to bless our children all the time, regardless of what it is, whether they get to go some place or we want to buy them something special or whatever. If in the middle of that planned blessing, they are just outright disobedient and full of rebellion, you have to withhold the blessing from them because it would look like we were blessing their disobedience. God is very much the same way.

He will withhold no good thing
from them that love him.

> For the LORD God *is* a sun and shield: the Lord will give grace and glory: no good *thing* will he withhold from them that walk uprightly. Psalm 84:11

Seek ye first the kingdom of God and His righteousness and then all these things shall be added unto you.

Anyone who leaves mother or father, husband or wife, children, houses or lands, because of the gospel shall be given in this life, mothers and fathers, brothers and sisters, houses and lands, an hundredfold and in the world to come, eternal life.

> [29]And Jesus answered and said, Verily I say unto you, There is no man that hath left house, or brethren, or sisters, or father, or mother, or wife, or children, or lands, for my sake, and the gospel's,

> ³⁰**But he shall receive an hundredfold now in this time, houses, and brethren, and sisters, and mothers, and children, and lands, with persecutions; and in the world to come eternal life.** Mark 10:29-30

How many are really leaving mother or father, husband or wife, brothers or sisters, or houses or lands in their heart for God. It doesn't mean you get divorced, it doesn't mean you leave your family. The context of this is: where are your priorities in your heart? It is not the external conclusion of the matter; it is the internal beginning of the matter.

Titus says, "These things speak and exhort and rebuke with all authority, and let no man despise thee." As a minister, I have to speak, I have to exhort, and I have to rebuke with all authority. "Let no man despise thee."

> ¹⁵**These things speak, and exhort, and rebuke with all authority.**
> ³:¹**Let no man despise thee. Put them in mind to be subject to principalities and powers, to obey magistrates, to be ready to every good work,**
> ²**To speak evil of no man, to be no brawlers, *but* gentle, shewing all meekness unto all men.**
> ³**For we ourselves also were sometimes foolish, disobedient, deceived, serving divers lusts and pleasures, living in malice and envy, hateful, *and* hating one another.** Titus 2:15-3:3

Watch your heart now! I only have your best interest at heart; I am not against you. That may come as a surprise to you. I am here for your benefit.

Put them in mind — the people you are speaking to, exhorting and rebuking with all authority. Put them in mind to be subject to the principalities and powers (not the satanic ones, but the godly, human ones). Put them in mind to be subject to the principalities and powers, to obey magistrates, to be ready to do every good work. To speak evil of no man, to be no brawlers, but gentle, showing all meekness unto all men. For we ourselves also were sometimes foolish, disobedient, deceived, serving divers lusts and pleasures, living in malice and envy, hateful, and hating one another.

"Ye adulterers and adulteresses, know ye not that the friendship with the world is enmity with God? Whosoever therefore will be a friend of the world is the enemy of God."

Do you think that the scriptures saith in vain, "The spirit that dwelleth in us lusteth to envy?" So Lust is tied into Envy.

> [4]Ye adulterers and adulteresses, know ye not that the friendship of the world is enmity with God? whosoever therefore will be a friend of the world is the enemy of God.
> [5]Do ye think that the scripture saith in vain, The spirit that dwelleth in us lusteth to envy? James 4:4-5

JEALOUSY IN THE JEWS

Why was Jesus killed? Because of Envy.

So then faith cometh by hearing and hearing by the Word of God. But I say, have they not heard? Yes, verily their sound went into all the earth and their words unto the ends of the world. But I say, didn't Israel know?

> [17]So then faith *cometh* by hearing, and hearing by the word of God.
> [18]But I say, Have they not heard? Yes verily, their sound went into all the earth, and their words unto the ends of the world.
> [19]But I say, Did not Israel know? First Moses saith, I will provoke you to jealousy by *them that are* no people, *and* by a foolish nation I will anger you.   Romans 10:17-19

This is talking about God. First Moses saith... Now here is the prophecy about the Jews going into apostasy and the Gentiles being grafted in. This is a direct quote from Deuteronomy 32:21, which says, "I will provoke you to jealousy by them that are no people. By a foolish nation I will anger you."

> They have moved me to jealousy with *that which is* not God; they have provoked me to anger with their vanities: and I will move them to jealousy with *those which are* not a people; I will provoke them to anger with a foolish nation.
> **Deuteronomy 32:21**

In today's society, the Jews hate the Gentiles who say they are right with God, and that is why they hate Christianity. It is because of Jesus; He is the rock of offense. He is the stumbling block. But pride and Envy and Jealousy are here. The Jews know they were God's chosen people. When anyone says otherwise or says that a Gentile is grafted in and becomes a son or daughter of God, calling God his Father, the Jews cannot accept it because of their Jealousy. Moses prophesied about their bad spirits long before they ever knew it.

What did Moses say? I will provoke you to Jealousy by them that are no people. There is a preeminence of Messianic Jews over born again Gentiles. I am going to get stoned for what I am about to say, but most Messianic congregations are prideful because there is a superiority attached to being a born again Jew. Paul dealt with that with Peter. Jesus dealt with it, and everyone dealt with it. There is neither Jew nor Greek in Christ. There is no distinction in the new creation between a born again Gentile and a born again Jew. We are one, and to teach otherwise is error. Number two, it is pride, and number three, it is Envy and Jealousy still working in the Jewish people over the Gentile issue, that Moses prophesied about in Deuteronomy 32.

> **There is neither Jew nor Greek, there is neither bond nor free, there is neither male nor female: for ye are all one in Christ Jesus.** Galatians 3:28

Not only did Moses do it, but Isaiah did too. Isaiah is very bold and saith, "I was found of them that sought me not; I was made manifest unto them that asked not after me. But to Israel He saith, all day long I have stretched forth my hands unto a disobedient and gainsaying people."

> **20But Esaias is very bold, and saith, I was found of them that sought me not; I was made manifest unto them that asked not after me.**
> **21But to Israel he saith, All day long I have stretched forth my hands unto a disobedient and gainsaying people.** Romans 10:20-21

> **1I am sought of them *that* asked not *for me;* I am found of them *that* sought me not: I said, Behold me, behold me, unto a nation *that* was not called by my name.**
> **2I have spread out my hands all the day unto a rebellious people, which walketh in a way *that was* not good, after their own thoughts;** Isaiah 65:1-2

Why did they kill Jesus? Out of Envy and Jealousy?

Matthew says,

> [15]Now at *that* feast the governor was wont to release unto the people a prisoner, whom they would.
> [16]And they had then a notable prisoner, called Barabbas.
> [17]Therefore when they were gathered together, Pilate said unto them, Whom will ye that I release unto you? Barabbas, or Jesus which is called Christ?
> [18]For he knew that for envy they had delivered him.
>
> Matthew 27:15-18

Listen to this. Jesus knew that they had delivered Him for Envy and Jealousy. When Envy and Jealousy is working, who links immediately with it? Bitterness. Who comes along to reinforce it? Bitterness. And what does Bitterness produce? Murder and all that stuff. Can you understand, when Jesus was hanging on the cross and He was about to die for you and me, why He made this incredible statement? "Father, forgive them, for they know not what they're doing."

What do you mean? Didn't they know what they were doing? No, they had gone down and this stuff was up. They were out of control and possessed with Bitterness and Jealousy and Covetousness and Envy. They were possessed of the devil, not Satan himself, but with the forces that answer to Satan that would produce this reality. So Christ was killed because of Envy.

Mark probably tells us the same thing.

> For he knew that the chief priests had delivered him for envy.   Mark 15:10

So who was behind the scenes, full of Envy? The spiritual leaders. Not just the people, but the leaders of God's people transferring Envy into them. This is called a transference of spirits. You have to be careful who you listen to. You need to be careful who you're around.

There could be a transference of evil spirits into you, to influence your thinking. That's why when someone speaks to you, and someone is operating around you, or you're in a casual conversation, you have to make sure there's a right spirit behind what they're speaking to you. Thoughts are contagious!

Do you know many people can come to you with scripture, and there's a wrong spirit behind it? Guess who appeared to Eve back in the garden in Genesis chapter 3. Satan. Did he come with or without the Word? He came with the Word.

When Jesus was being tempted, who appeared to Jesus? Satan. Did he come with or without the Word? But behind it was a wrong spirit. There has to be a right spirit, and that right spirit has to be linked up with the Holy Spirit which is a revealer of all truth according to the Word of God. The religious leaders had a wrong spirit.

You and I today as Christians are a source of Envy and Jealousy and Bitterness and hatred to the Jewish nation. The Christians have not helped this hatred either, because of the Catholics and the Christians in the great crusades against the Jews. They have not forgotten, either. So now today, anti-Semitism is as strong in the church as it is in the world. But as Israel is blessed, so I am blessed. The Psalm says to pray for the peace of Jerusalem.

> **Pray for the peace of Jerusalem: they shall prosper that love thee.** Psalm 122:6

Who lives in Jerusalem? The Jews. They shall prosper that love thee. Do you want to have a curse on your head? Persecute the Jews. "But," you say, "They are apostate." Okay, wild vine, what is your case? Except for the grace of God, so go you. The Bible says that if God spared not the true vine, what is the case of the wild vine that errs? As a wild vine, appreciate the true vine you came from by faith.

The Word says that salvation is of the Jews. Salvation is from the true vine, the seed of Abraham, by faith. Gentiles are grafted in as a wild vine.

> Ye worship ye know not what: we know what we worship: for salvation is of the Jews. John 4:22

> ¹⁶For if the firstfruit *be* holy, the lump *is* also *holy:* and if the root *be* holy, so *are* the branches.
> ¹⁷And if some of the branches be broken off, and thou, being a wild olive tree, wert graffed in among them, and with them partakest of the root and fatness of the olive tree;
> ¹⁸Boast not against the branches. But if thou boast, thou bearest not the root, but the root thee.
> ¹⁹Thou wilt say then, The branches were broken off, that I might be graffed in.
> ²⁰Well; because of unbelief they were broken off, and thou standest by faith. Be not highminded, but fear:
> ²¹For if God spared not the natural branches, *take heed* lest he also spare not thee.
> ²²Behold therefore the goodness and severity of God: on them which fell, severity; but toward thee, goodness, if thou continue in *his* goodness: otherwise thou also shalt be cut off.
> ²³And they also, if they abide not still in unbelief, shall be graffed in: for God is able to graff them in again.
> ²⁴For if thou wert cut out of the olive tree which is wild by nature, and wert graffed contrary to nature into a good olive tree: how much more shall these, which be the natural branches, be graffed into their own olive tree? Romans 11:16-24

Second Corinthians says, "Would to God you could bear with me a little in my folly, and indeed bear with me. For I am jealous over you with godly jealousy." Now here is that godly counterpart, that zeal of care. This is Paul speaking to the church at Corinth by the very same spirit of God that would be in godly jealousy. This is kind of the way I feel. If you could hear my heart right now, my heart beats with Paul. For I am jealous over you with godly jealousy, for I have espoused you to one husband, the Lord Jesus, that I may present you as a chaste virgin to Christ. But I fear, lest by any means... Paul is saying that divination is going to come. But I am afraid that as the serpent beguiled Eve through his subtlety, which was divination, so your mind could be corrupted from the simplicity that is in Christ. For if he that cometh preacheth another Jesus, another gospel, another testament, that we have not preached, or if ye receive another spirit, which you have not received from us, this would be the wrong spirit, another gospel, a false religion or false gospel that does not bear the witness of scripture.

> ¹Would to God ye could bear with me a little in *my* folly: and indeed bear with me.
> ²For I am jealous over you with godly jealousy: for I have espoused you to one husband, that I may present *you as* a chaste virgin to Christ.
> ³But I fear, lest by any means, as the serpent beguiled Eve through his subtilty, so your minds should be corrupted from the simplicity that is in Christ.
> ⁴For if he that cometh preacheth another Jesus, whom we have not preached, or *if* ye receive another spirit, which ye have not received, or another gospel, which ye have not accepted, ye might well bear with *him.*   2 Corinthians 11:1-4

It goes on to talk about how he was the chiefest of sinners. The thrust of this is to win men to Christ in a simplistic manner, not forgetting what you have been called from, what you have been called to and what you have been pledged to.

"Envy and Jealousy" has to be on your hit list. Covetousness has to be on your hit list because it feeds Envy and Jealousy. The scriptures bear witness to that. Rejection also feeds Envy and Jealousy and it feeds into Bitterness. That is not the way God created you from the foundation of the world, and you need to be free.

You are a very privileged people to even have spiritual understanding given to you because the world is running around and does not have the foggiest idea what is going on. They don't know why they are all goofed up and in trouble.

MINISTRY LIST

We are going into a place before the Lord where we will take responsibility for our lives in the areas that we are dealing with, which is the spirit of Jealousy and the spirit of Envy and Jealousy, as well as Covetousness and greed. Some of these are tied into Bitterness. Now I want to go down through a list of things and as I go down through this list, I want you to mentally and spiritually make a note if you have had a problem with this, or are having a problem with this, or your family tree has ever had a problem with this because these are underlings. Remember, Ephesians 6:12 says that our battle is not with flesh and blood, but with principalities, powers, spiritual wickedness in high places, the rulers of the darkness of this world. There is a four-tiered bureaucracy that is working. It is a structured system that is designed to control you and make you a medium of expression.

You are going to make your list and go before the Lord and say, "I want this out of my life." Do you think cruelty is part of the nature of God? Have you ever found people being cruel to other people, just spontaneously growling? Mark these down if you want to deal with them. How about fury? Fury would be anger and wrath maxed out. That is an insane anger, destructively so. Malice, sadism. Do you know that there is something in some people that wants to abuse? There is also something within other people that will go out of the way to make people reject them so that there can be that sadism. Screaming is a form of retaliation coming out of Envy and Jealousy. Spitefulness. Treachery. Malice is a form of hatred, keeping a record of wrongs to the degree that you are the Orkin man. It is the basis for extermination. That is all coming out of retaliation. I am including retaliation because it is all entwined now with Envy and Jealousy. Masochism is self-destructive, to the persecuted and the victim. People going into rages scream at each other as a form of retaliation. That is a get even defense mechanism coming out of Bitterness.

STEALING

Stealing comes out of Envy and Covetousness. Kleptomania, which is basically shoplifting, is a very interesting one because it is rooted in self-hatred. Individuals who are compulsive in buying and spending to be fulfilled are rooted deeply in self-rejection and self-hatred. Kleptomania is related to compulsive spending, coming out of Envy and Jealousy and Covetousness. It is linked this time by an Unloving spirit of self-rejection and self-hatred. There is a need to be fulfilled.

These groupings of principalities have tentacles that reach out and link with each other. So we are not trying to set a whole bunch of things in order; we are just trying to show you some things that would be linking that I think you might need to deal with today in conjunction with Envy and Jealousy and where Bitterness comes in.

TREACHERY

Spitefulness is retaliation. Treachery is even more dangerous because it is a subtle, deceptive conniving in which people appear to love you, but behind the scenes they are looking to overthrow you and destroy you. People who are filled with treachery will get around you like a friend, just to gather information about you so they can turn against you later. That is classic treachery.

CRAVING

When we talk about craving,
we are not talking about food.

Greed would be craving; craving would be greed. The word "insatiable" would be closely tied to it: a compulsive need to have. Keeping up with the Joneses would be close to craving, rooted in competition, rooted in Envy and Jealousy.

NEED TO KNOW

There is nothing wrong with curiosity, but there is a side to curiosity that can be dangerous. We call that the "need to know"; those who have it are "the knowing ones." The need to know comes out of matriarchal witchcraft. The need to know is rooted in Occultism. But in the area of Envy and Jealousy, the need to know is a spiritual dimension where people do not want to be left out of anything that is going on, because of Covetousness. They just do not want to be left out. Have you ever seen people who just have to be involved? They have to know everything you are doing. They have to know everything you have. They just have to know, and they are not satisfied until they know everything about you. What they cannot get from you, they will go around to your friends and find out what they know about you so that they can be satisfied that you don't have an edge over them. That is rooted in Covetousness and greed, and Envy.

DISCONTENTMENT

Another area of Covetousness and Envy and Jealousy is being discontent. This means not being at peace every day. It means that restlessness, that constant sifting of agitation, that constant feeling of never being satisfied, always scanning, always looking. It is looking around and saying, "What did I miss? I missed something." Having to be on top of everything is coming out of Envy and Jealousy. Occultism is also linked with that. In Occultism we call those people "the knowing ones." They just have a need to know everything. Well, you know what? You don't have to have a need to know everything. There are just some things that are none of your business. Envy and Jealousy and Covetousness are rooted in discontent.

PRIDE OF LIFE

Material lust is another one. That is pride of life, which is fixing your desires and your hopes and your dreams on material, materialistic things. Materialistic society has pride of life; keeping up with the Joneses is pride of life. You have to look a certain way. You have to act a certain way. You have to go to the right country clubs, hang around with the right people, who drive the right cars and wear the right type of designer label clothing. You must look the part, speak the part, act the part. In fact, it is the epitome of what would be considered materialistic success. That is pride of life. Anyone can have it. It doesn't have to be someone who is successful. Pride of life can be found at any level of existence. Everyone has hopes and desires. We aren't talking about hopes because everyone has the right to believe for God's blessing and for the things of life. We aren't talking about a poverty mentality. We are talking about someone with this type of mentality who is obsessed with success, obsessed with looking around and comparing themselves. We are not talking about basic desires. There is nothing wrong with wanting a new car or home or whatever. That is not the same thing. Pride of life would be a driving obsession, a compelling mindset that would drive the person to compete at all levels.

Driven to succeed

because of the fear of poverty

With the Jews, the pride of life is where they are so driven. In their mentality, you are not really a Jew unless you are a professional who is highly visible in the professions where money can be made, as a part of one's life. That is pride of life coming out of Envy and Jealousy and Covetousness. The sad thing about the Jews is that they do not have to worry about it too much because God promised Abraham that He would bless him and bless his seed. God is doing that even in their apostasy.

CLOSING PRAYER

We want to come before the Lord who is invisible in the heavenlies, who is here by the Holy Spirit. Have your hearts been convicted by the teaching? We have had some reflection but all of it is meaningless if it doesn't make a change in our hearts. Amen? I want Envy and Jealousy to be gone from my life. How about you? I don't want it to feed Bitterness, and I don't want it to cause this junk to have anything to do with my life. I don't want anything to do with Covetousness. I don't want anything to do with Envy and Jealousy.

> Father, this is a special time. We have been before You searching our hearts and our family trees and our personal lives. We don't want to be a hearer of the Word only, but we want to be a doer also. Father, as we come before You, the Father of all spirits, we want you to know that we are not rebels; we are obedient spirits. Once we were disobedient spirits; now we are obedient spirits. Father, I ask You in the name of the Lord Jesus Christ to deliver every humble and contrite one here from the powerful forces of Covetousness and Envy and Jealousy along with any lingering spirits of Bitterness and retaliation, resentment, unforgiveness, that may not have left already because of Envy and Jealousy. When Envy and Jealousy is dealt with, the power of these lingering spirits will also be broken so that there is no linking or networking here behind the scenes that would produce these powerful forces of resentment, allowing Bitterness to get a foothold.

> Father, search our hearts today. Let's not look at the other person and say, "Well, I know they

125

have it, but not me, bless God." I know what Paul said, that if a brother be overtaken in a fault, those of you who consider yourself spiritual, restore such an one in the spirit of meekness and consider yourself also, lest you be tempted in like manner and fall away.

Brethren, if a man be overtaken in a fault, ye which are spiritual, restore such an one in the spirit of meekness; considering thyself, lest thou also be tempted. Galatians 6:1

Every one of us is susceptible to Covetousness, Father. It is in the world, it's all around us. Every one of us, Father, is susceptible to Envy and Jealousy. It's in the world, it's all around us, and it even may be part of us. Father, deliver us. Let Your glory be manifest in our hearts. If there be any evil thing within us, take it from us today, in this area, as we submit our life to You. Father, as we prepare our hearts to repent to You, as we prepare our hearts to receive Your forgiveness and Your deliverance, I ask that You would do it sovereignly. Let Your Spirit touch every person.

All the people said, Amen.

Someone has to set the standard in this earth. Who would you suggest it be? The guy next door? The guy down the street? It begins with each of us. It hurts so badly to be separated in the area of relationship. That is why the devil comes and makes it his number one object of war against you, and he knows how to get you. God created you to be vulnerable. One of the greatest evidences of healing is when you can be exposed to this stuff in others and not be personally affected, yet remain vulnerable without hardness. Could you be vulnerable with every opportunity to be scarred and yet remain soft and precious? Envy and Jealousy will prevent relationship because it's a killer.

Envy and Jealousy has to go.

Are your hearts now prepared to come before the Lord? I am going to lead you in a prayer before God. Come, bring your hearts before the Lord.

> Father, I come to You in the name of Jesus, to know the truth. You said the truth will make us free. Let the convicting power of the Holy Spirit bring to my remembrance the things that I have read, the concepts and the precepts that will be a standard for my righteousness. Take Envy and Jealousy from me today, God. Take from me the wandering eyes that look at others and that would feed into Rejection and Bitterness. I release every person, out of a simple obedience to You. I release every person to you, and I release myself to you. Purge me with hyssop, and make me clean. Deliver me from the spirits of Covetousness, and the spirits of Envy and Jealousy. Take them from me today, God. I do not want them. They are not good for my brother and they are not good for me. Amen.

> Father, I acknowledge that in my generations my family tree has been filled with Covetousness and Envy and Jealousy, and the curse of it has flowed generation to generation. It is linked with Bitterness, linked with Rejection, linked with pride. I want it gone. I want to be free of the curse of my ancestors. I want the curse of iniquities passing down three to four generations, in Exodus 20:5, to be broken in my life. I want to be released, and I

thank You through Jesus Christ that I can be released today. I receive it and I accept it in the name of the Lord Jesus Christ. I accept my freedom from ancestral curses. I accept my freedom from personal curses.

Envy and Jealousy, I have a perfect hatred for you. Just as there is a godly counterpart to jealousy, there is a godly counterpart to hatred and the hatred that I have is a holy one. You are not acceptable in my life. I fall out of agreement with you Jealousy, I fall out of agreement with you Envy. I fall out of agreement with you Covetousness. I want nothing to do with you. I discern you. I see you, and I know you. I have discernment so I resist you, and you shall flee from my life this day. In the name of Jesus, Amen.

INDEX

SCRIPTURE INDEX